SIMPLY SCEN

An Insight into the Art of Landscape Modelling

By Tony Hill

IRWELL

PRESS

i

All hands to the fore! Modellers weekend in Blairgowrie '93. Photograph Bill Roberton.

**First Published in the United Kingdom by
IRWELL PRESS 1995
P.O.Box 1260, Caernarfon, Gwynedd, LL55 3ZD
Printed in Huddersfield by The Amadeus Press**

CONTENTS

Introduction
**An Insight into the
Art of Landscape Modelling** 5

Chapter One
Setting Out in the Right Direction 14

Chapter Two
Basic Landscaping
*Building a Foundation for your Landscape,
Contouring and Texturing* 18

Chapter Three
On the Rocks 30

Chapter Four
At the Grass Roots 36

Chapter Five
Growing Your Own Trees 46

Chapter Six
Water, Water, Everywhere 57

Chapter Seven
Walls and Hedges 62

Chapter Eight
Conclusion 70

Acknowledgements

Dedicated to Sue and Jason, who set the ball rolling

All sequential photographs Graham Baseden,
whose patience seemed unending!!
Other photos:Len Weal,
Peter Barnfield, Bill Roberton.
Special thanks to Brian & Pat Champion (Set Scenes),
The Tuesday Night 'Mafia',
Exhibition Managers up and down the country,
Malcolm Dunstall, and a special thanks to Peter (my neighbour)
for the loan of his word processor.

The railway in its natural setting amongst trees, grass, hills and water, and the wonderful Monsal Dale Viaduct over the Wye. Remember, geology shapes the land and in the area of The Peak the limestone lays flat in layer after layer (see Headstone Tunnel, page 6) to give the characteristic flat-topped hills, broken and incised by fast flowing rivers.

Introduction

An Insight into the Art of LANDSCAPE MODELLING

Although my threats to produce this book were for years considered idle, I have at last put pen to paper and exposed to critical glare the various collected techniques employed in my landscape modelling. They are by no means all my own ideas but a combination, that has been put (sometimes thrown) together and adapted to suit my style of modelling. It must be said that little has been written in recent years about the art of creating realistic landscapes, as a step by step approach. This book has been based on my methods demonstrated at exhibitions, honed and developed over the last few years, which started out as Tree Making and blossomed (literally) into the elaborate full scenic landscape demonstrations that I do today.

I first became interested in modelling landscapes when I built a model railway for my son as a Christmas present back in 1977, and my wife suggested that I join the local model railway club, Folkestone, Hythe and District MRC, to see how other modellers created their railways. At the club I met Dick Wyatt of Dovey Valley fame who guided me through the basics, and I was then introduced to the artistic prowess of Neil Tanner. These two men were the most important influences in my early years of modelling.

It has been said that you need to have an artistic bent to model landscapes - that may well be so, but I feel that we are all capable of producing plausible scenery, through some simple methods. The aim of this book is to cover the very broad subject of scenic modelling, as simply as possible, using readily available materials. Artistry or not, to model a landscape that is realistic and representative does need a lot of thought (I hesitate to say groundwork) and a fair bit of research, which need not be a laborious exercise when conducted as part of a holiday or a week-end away from it all. The family may not even suspect what you are up to. I find it a good idea to have a camera with me at such times, taking as many snapshots of a given area as I possibly can, and noting the types of trees, colour of rocks (if there are rocks exposed) colour of soil, types of hedges, fences and stone walls if any. I also carry with me a pocket book in which to note species of trees, though a reference work is needed

Huntsman's Cottage, Mount Edgcumbe. W7696.

Mother nature takes hold. Apart from the grand sweep of hills, most of the homely elements of Simply Scenery *are here, in this photograph.*

Drystone walls rising almost vertically. Phew! A piece of stonewalling so dramatic that unless proof such as this existed, a modeller would probably dismiss it as improbable, and not attempt it. The 0-6-0 is emerging from Headstone Tunnel onto Monsal Dale Viaduct - the rock is quite obviously horizontal (or 'flat lying') with each layer or stratum one above the other. For the natural world, this is unusually uniform and when modelling of course, each rock layer need not be the same thickness as its neighbour - far from it. Photograph D. Ibbotson.

for this - there are some books - see Chapter 8 - currently available, and these are detailed elsewhere. They are packed full of colour illustrations, leaf formations, heights, where you will find what growing, types of bark, colour and texture

and all the rest. If you do get a species subtly wrong, comfort yourself that few will ever notice, the prototype could have appeared by the hand of man in any event (what price monkey puzzles, eucalyptus and the rest?) and in any case you've

assisted the spread of a species - your own part in the Darwinian process...

It is also necessary to note the way the hills and valleys run; the railway engineers used the land for embankments and cuttings, taking the soil from the

Classic bare rock cutting. Grass attempts to colonise from above, attaching itself to any less-than vertical niche, while the material which inevitably crumbles off the bare face piles up at the base, forming a further, more gently sloped and more hospitable home for veg. Remember these natural processes - it's all gravity really. Model railways in their neatness often miss these subtleties.

Engineers, or rather the navigators, moved massive amounts of earth to obtain level ground such as at Ambergate, that delightful Derbyshire triangular station. Note the scale of the distant vista and the scale relationship as the land runs away to the horizon. This could be a model backdrop! Note also the tremendous variation to be found even in a small area - woods, trimmed hedges, rough hedges, hedges with trees, rough grass, cut grass, corn, cut corn, gardens, fences, walls, shrubs, bushes - well that's enough to go on with...

higher ground and using it to fill the smaller valleys. Gravity was their friend and bearing this in mind when modelling will make all the difference between a model railway on a flat baseboard, and a realistic model railway running realistically through countryside. Nature formed the land and the engineers shifted it to suit their needs. It is true to say that most us of will spend a great deal of time making locomotives and rolling stock, railway buildings and even towns, but have relatively little time for the land beyond the railway fence - a sweeping statement I know, but it has relevance. You should know that whatever your model's setting, if it is to have some 'truth' it will obey the same 'rules', constraints and moulding influences of geology, climate, farming practice and so on that apply in the real countryside. Obeying

Trees, rock, water and walls in abandon. This is The Peak between Cressbrook and Litton Tunnels - spot the tiny portion of railway!

More broken ground altogether - harder, more variable rocks and a tougher history of ice and wind. Trees have a much poorer living to make in the Highlands - this is believed to be near Morar. Loco is Mogul No.61788 LOCH RANNOCH. Photograph N. Stead Collection.

these simple ordinances, which I hesitate (again) to call ground rules, will avoid limestone crags on a Great Eastern branch, or granite tors in a Midlands valley. I will now endeavour to set some details in place by taking a look at various regions of our country -

SCOTLAND

The Scottish landscape can be divided into three distinct areas, the Highlands, the Central Lowlands and the Borders, divided from England and from each other by vast geological fault systems.
The Highlands

More rugged Scottish terrain. Remember that our forebears, working and often dying in these hostile climes, were hardly likely to remove the debris for the sake of cosmetics, unless it was wanted for fill further along the line. Rocks blasted for the headland now underlie the train and protect it from the sea loch. Photograph P.J. Lynch.

Drystone walls need not inhabit the open country... Photograph E.R. Morten.

A mainly rough and rugged rocky landscape, with high mountains, moors and fells and deep valleys (open and often U shaped in their cross section - a consequence of glaciation). A river valley which has not enjoyed the doubtful advantage of a glacier bulging through its length, will have a characteristic V shape). Few trees grow except in the narrow valleys where there are Douglas Fir and Scots Pines, and a few Sessile Oaks. The northern and easterly parts of the Highlands are windblown with mile upon mile of heather. The west side tends to be more rugged with long, intricate sea lochs (essentially fiords - again a consequence of glaciation), deep inland lochs and craggy outcrops of rock. Boulder-strewn scree slopes characterise many outcrops and many large (often very large) exposed outcrops, particularly in valley floors, are rounded and polished smooth by ice action.

The photograph of course was taken to record the much more (to the photographer) interesting derailment - the spoil heap (or bing if we're in Scotland) is a man-made landscape which is disappearing from the country now but used to be found wherever the earth was mined, from Cornwall to Scotland. Slate waste, of course, makes a different shape - and is likely to stay around longer. In nature, with its much greater timescales, such conical forms are hardly ever found - only, funny enough, in volcanic or very cold, permafrost terrains. The 'slag heap' is not complete without the striking gullies (called rills) carved into it by rainwater run-off. The surface, unconsolidated and too steep, is constantly shifting and plants find it hard to get a grip - hence the 'greening' of tips has often not taken place, even decades later. Photograph P.J. Lynch.

The mighty oak on the village green is only one in a multiplicity of tree forms - what could be further from that idealised English tree than a yew clinging to a crag? Below is The Peak line, climbing north at 1 in 90, leaving Rusher Cutting Tunnel to cross the river.

Central Lowlands

This area is heavily populated, has mountains with grassy slopes, lochs of great beauty and broad plains with towns and cities within. There used to be much heavy industry but in recent years this has diminished, allowing for mother nature to take a hold again. Trees are more common with Ash, Aspens, Birches, Alders and Oaks. There is a lot of scope for landscaping here, so you can vary the modelling within a small distance, and I am sure it will look right.

The Borders

Much more rolling countryside here but still with moorlands and lochs and a great opportunity for a 'wide open' approach to modelling. A greater variety of trees and shrubs, common species of trees as above, together with Wych Elms by streams and rivers, Willows (not necessarily weeping) and Rowans.

ENGLAND

In a rather lordly and certainly arbitrary fashion, for the purposes of this introduction I've divided England up into North, South, East, West and Midlands.

The wonderfully evocative limestone country around Buxton is a challenge for any landscape modeller - this is the curve through Miller Dale, with a freight being banked.

Far more homely setting - trees alongside the Wisbech & Upwell tramway - note just how close we can bring our trees onto the line. There is a prototype for everything...

The North

The Lakes and parts of the North West can be said to constitute a mini Scotland with a similar variety of mountains, rolling hills, deep valleys, lakes, rivers and streams, with trees of all the common types from Hawthorns to Great Oaks. Dry stone walls abound. It is far wetter here than across the Pennines on the east side, so the grass will be green and lush, supporting dairy herds and sheep. In the North East livestock farming is predominant and on the high moors stone walls have pride of place. Hedgerows are more common on the lower plains leading towards the North Sea. As it is a dryer area more crops are grown. The countryside abounds with trees such as Sessile Oak, Ash, Hazel and Sycamore, and closer to the Border areas are plantations of quick growing Firs, edged with Silver Birch trees. It should be noted also that Oak trees are more common on the roadside and in amongst the hedgerows in the more open landscape. The Pennines split England in two, a barren landscape with miles of heather, peat and outcrops of rock. There are many streams and small rivers which in years past were a source of power for mill

Mother nature's not quite arrived yet! All railways were new at one time - this is the brand new Amesbury branch (at Newton Tony?) confounding our notions of how effortlessly railways blend into the countryside they serve.

Embankment veg. again - so much variety in what is a relatively restricted area. I might just use that backdrop one day... Photograph J.J. Smith.

machinery. Photography here is very important if you want to capture 'the look'.

The Midlands

This area really is diverse in landscape terms. Derbyshire has the Peaks with limestone gorges and high open tracts of land, plenty of tree lined roads and densely wooded hillsides. Red sandstone is common to the West Midlands, weathered down to give that lovely rich red soil. Hard rocky outcrops overlook the plain of the lower Severn with its heavily wooded valley walls of Ash, Sycamore, Oak and Silver Birch. To the north are areas of volcanic rock; rivers play a great

part in the look of the landscape, with the two vast drainage systems of the Trent and the Severn, all running through a huge variety of landscapes, with trees such as Oak, Elm, Beech, Ash, Birch, and many more.

Eastern England

Flat - well, flattish - chalk and claylands, with fertile lands eminently suitable for cereal crops. The hills are often tree covered, and between them are miles of 'flats' with drainage channels, so there is an opportunity for great variety in your modelling. Trees such as Crack Willow, Weeping Willow, Walnuts, Ash, Elms (if you can find any), Birches, Oaks both

Sessile and Old English abound. Crack Willow, being pollarded gives quite a distinctive appearance. Much of the land is carpeted with glacial material, a clay full of flints and boulders - this has imparted much of the gentle rolling quality of the landscape, masking the 'sharp edges'. 'Constable skies' are all you need to bear in mind for the modelling background to much of this slice of England. Slow rivers have enormous modelling potential, especially at low tide, shrinking to little more than a stream wandering through expanses of mud and silt on the banks.

Southern England

The South East is well known for its chalk downs and farmland, with woods of Oaks and Beeches, Silver Birch and Ash. Hawthorns, Alders, both Crack and Weeping Willow and Sycamore, vie with Hazel and Hornbeam in hedgerows lining the country lanes, along with the odd Sessile Oak and Sycamore. Kent and East Sussex both boast marshland, whilst north Kent has chalky outcrops which were and are exploited for cement - great modelling potential for narrow gauge enthusiasts here. Flint is common and is used in buildings to great effect.

Towards Southampton there are still chalk downlands and beyond of course is the New Forest. There are sands and clays, with Scots Pines, Hemlock, Alders, Silver Birch, and Oaks the most common trees. Wiltshire with the Salisbury Plain (which is far from flat) has a thin soil coverage, therefore sheep farming and cereal crops are common.

The other end of Mother Nature's spectrum. Trees do not always grow in an Eden ...

Photos like these are of course useful - vital - for detailing a model - that's why they're here, of course. Books and magazines contain, somewhere, most of the inspiration we need - often unintentionally. A unique image of some rare piece of stock, the apple of some wagoneer's eye, can be cheerfully ignored by us and attention focused on the really interesting bit - the adjacent bush, maybe... At this point I have been ordered to recommend you buy British Railways Illustrated and Modelling Railways Illustrated for scenes like this. It is, incidentally, Aberbeeg shed on the Western Region, in the 1950s.

The West

Like Britain as a whole, each region enjoys enormous variety, from the Mendips to the peaty flats of the Levels, and some of the most attractive hills and rock outcrops are found in the West Country. Only here do the hedgerows still divide up the land like a patchwork quilt. The little valleys of Exmoor are sharply incised into red sandstones, whilst Dartmoor owes its singular tors to the vast underlying body of granite - a distinctive white granite at that. There are few trees except in the fertile valleys. Further south on the Channel approaches the soil is red in colour denoting sandstone again. In Cornwall there are clay deposits, which give those huge waste heaps - making in turn for exciting modelling opportunities.

WALES

South Wales with its rolling Brecons and deep valleys, in years past were filled with heavy industry. Bereft of large trees, in recent years there seems to have been something of a replanting, with small Oaks and Silver Birches appearing and copses springing up everywhere. Observations when walking the old track beds will give you a good idea of what has been before. In Mid and North Wales, rock outcrops are much more common, along with slate spoil heaps. The grass is very green of course, because of the enormous amounts of rain - most of which comes during my holidays. Stone walls, as many

of them derelict as there are in use, go everywhere up and over mountains, with slate slabs forming railway fences along some of the track beds. There are wooded valleys with fast flowing rivers skirting the valley floor. Trees tend to be smaller and more compact, with Oaks, Birches, Wych Elms and Hawthorns the most common.

I hope this ludicrously brief look (sorry to sound like an Intourist guide) at our lovely country will give you an incentive to go out with your cameras, tree identification book and notebook and

really take in the nature that is around; it will certainly help to successfully model the landscape in which your railway will run. Always remember that the prototype itself offers almost limitless variety. Nowhere in the world is such geological and scenic variation found in such a limited area as in the British Isles, and there are still branch line trips, even today, which take you from flat drowned coastal mudlands to high moors with wind-stunted trees and bushes, within a few miles.

Grass growing despite the worst efforts of man ...

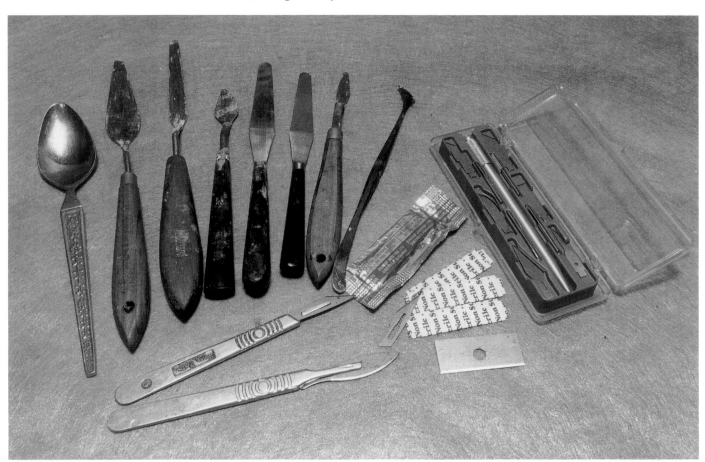

The range of tools - pallet knives, although not essential, are useful - an old butterknife will serve the purpose admirably in their absence..

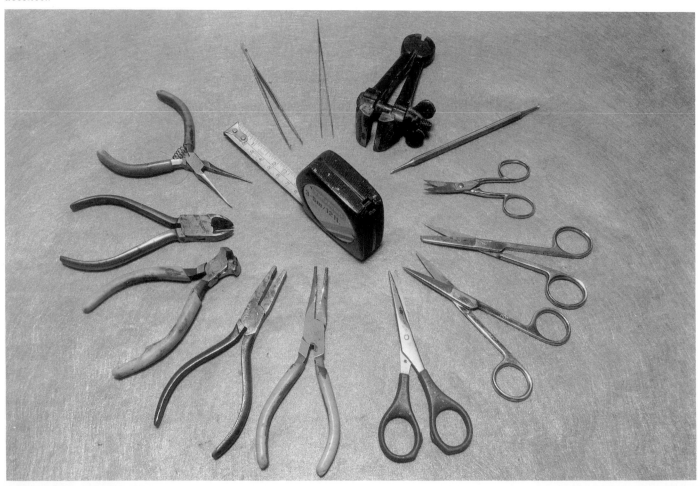

Chapter One
SETTING OUT IN THE RIGHT DIRECTION

As with any hobby, good basic tools are the foundation on which we can build our empire. For example, when constructing an etched brass kit you would use a good soldering iron, flux and a good solder; the essential scenic modelling equivalents are a good craft knife, straight edge, and pencil. The following list, although fairly comprehensive, is nevertheless a guide only. It is not exhaustive, and you may find other tools that are useful. I am only too aware of the cost of some items, but you can find many (or their equivalent) much cheaper at Model Railway Exhibitions, from the specialist traders that currently inhabit 'the circuit'.

Tools

Pencils of varying grades, not too hard, 3B to HB is about the best.

Felt tip pens, black, green, blue in colour with a wide tip are ideal for marking out profiles.

A straight edge, preferably a stainless steel type, 1 metre in length.

A metric or imperial rule, again stainless steel, and/or boxwood.

A craft knife or Swan Norton scalpel holder; a No.3 or 4 will be sufficient.

Tweezers, straight spoon-ended and crank-ended type.

An old screwdriver with a flat end, not the crosshead type, preferably an old electrical 'driver.

Coping saw, or even a power jigsaw.

Old Dentists probes. These are not essential but are very useful for detailed work on rockfaces and stonewalls.

A 25 watt soldering iron - something like an Antex 'S' with a heatsink/holder is ideal.

A small gas blow torch, though not essential, is very handy for the heavy gauge copper wire used in tree making.

Solder. I have been using Drapers solder but a 45 degree uncored wire solder is more user friendly.

A good flux. 12% phosphoric acid flux is about the best for our purposes.

A hot melt glue gun, look for the type with a trigger application as these are far easier to use. There are cheaper types available without a trigger but they are very much harder to use, as the glue stick will have to be pushed through the heating element with the aid of your thumb - this results in a profound ache in your prime digit after about five minutes.

Bostik and Bosch are two of the well known manufacturers, and you can find these in most big DIY Superstores, ranging in price from around £10 upwards. Glue sticks for these guns come in 10mm diameter and in varying lengths and the best type is the general purpose one, which can be clear or opaque.

A small hand-held vice or bench modellers vice with screw fixings.

Paint brushes. A good half inch decorator's brush and various artists type brushes, such as squirrel hair and the new generation acrylic bristle, are ideal.

Small artist's palette knives, ranging in lengths and widths, come in useful though they are not entirely essential - an old butter knife will do. (Confession: I use the latter for general landscape work.)

An old coffee grinder, electrical type, or come to that an old liquidiser. It is essential to have the consent of the domestic authority before using these items for modelling purposes.

A small hand held hairdryer. 850 watt will be adequate.

Various sizes of plastic mixing bowls, like those used for microwave cooking.

Several pairs of scissors, varying in size

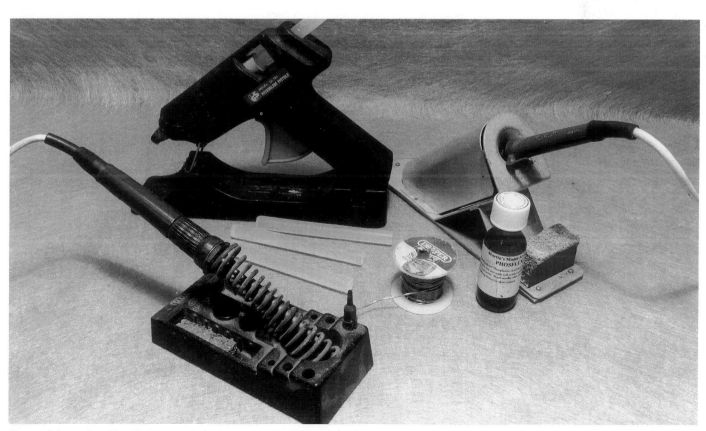

Some of the tools - Glue Gun, 15 and 24 watt soldering irons.

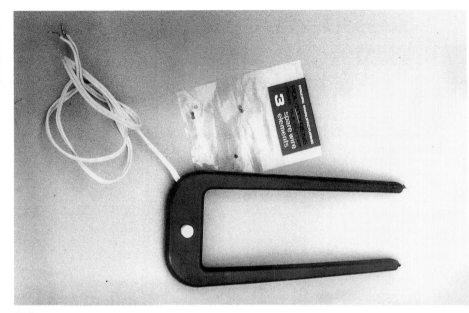

Polystyrene cutter.

from kitchen scissors down to nail scissors.

Safety Precautions
As with all tools, you must be careful how you use them. Keep them clean and they will last, but mistreat them and you will be forever replacing them. When using sharp tools, such as a craft knife or scalpel, always keep your fingers behind the cutting edge. I know it sounds elementary but I do say this from bitter experience. As an apprentice joiner working at the bench I had my knuckles wrapped more than once, by the old boys (now I'm one) for not obeying this simple rule. One day the inevitable happened - I was working on my own, paring a shoulder to a tenon after sharpening the chisel, which slipped when the timber rolled after I had applied too much pressure. I very efficiently removed most of the top of my index finger on my left hand, and still suffer to this day. This accident happened some 27 years ago, so be warned.

The same rules apply when using a hot glue gun, always keep your hands well clear of the molten glue. It is useful to have a pot of cold water handy - if you do burn your fingers dip them in the cold water (and keep them there) to take away the heat from the skin.

As an added safety precaution when using electricity, a good circuit breaker of the plug-in type is a must.

Materials
Again this is not an exhaustive list, for every scenic modeller will come across something new or different, and for this reason alone it is the worst hobby for inducing that 'never throw anything away habit'. What follows is at least usually available free or at a modest cost:

Corrugated cardboard boxes, the type with the two surface faces.

Cereal boxes, preferably empty.

Newspaper.

Tissue paper, either kitchen towel, or the industrial paper hand towels.

Plywood, 3mm-6mm.

Decorative ceiling plaster, generally known as Artex.

PVA glue. Rowney make a craft PVA glue which is much cheaper than the woodworking kind.

Resin W - which is an enhanced PVA glue and is water resistant.

Copydex. A latex glue.

Unscented Hairspray, firm or extra firm hold. I tend to use the pump action type now as they are more controllable i.e. the amount that you use is not governed by a gas propellant, but by your finger pressure.

Felt carpet underlay - the hairy kind, which is available from such people as Set Scenes of Crawley or, if you are lucky, from carpet suppliers. I tend to favour the natural coloured type rather than the dark brown variety which has to be bleached.

Glues to the left - paints to the right!

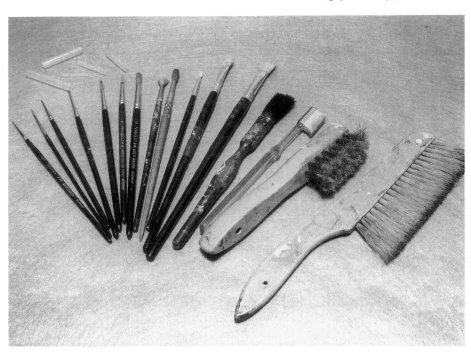

A variety of brushes I find very useful.

Various scatter materials - usually of the crushed latex kind, available from such suppliers as Set Scenes and Greenscene.
Surgical Lint - this can be expensive and has limited use.
Sisal string.
Plumbers hemp.
Old brush bristles.
Household electrical wire, preferably of the multi-stranded type (more of this later).
Expanded polystyrenes - packaging used by electrical component manufacturers, ceiling tiles, or cavity wall insulation slabs known as Jablite. This product is available from Builders' Merchants and varies in thickness from 1 inch to 6 inches, and up to 8 ft x 4 ft in sheet size.
Insulation board, sometimes known as Tentest board, available again from Builders' Merchants. It comes in 8 ft x 4 ft x 5/8th sheets.
Rubberised horsehair, useful for hedgerows, tree foliage carrier and shrubs.
Pot Scourers of the foam back kind, from your local Supermarket.
Polyester fibre - this is the stuffing of cushions, anoraks, quilts and so on, and is also supplied by Set Scenes and Greenscenes. It serves in various ways for ground cover, shrubs and trees.
Postiche, also known as dolls hair or crepe hair. Really it is an artificial theatrical hair and comes in various colours, from grey through to blonde to black - it's available from Set Scenes, joke shops (be careful here as they supply a straightened kind, not suited to our purposes) and theatrical costumieres. It serves as a foliage carrier on trees, shrubs etc.
DAS, an air drying modelling clay available from most art shops and good model shops.

Industrial floor scrubber discs, the kind used on those enormous floor polishers. These exotic things serve for hedges, shrubs and tree foliage and can be obtained (used) from contract cleaning companies, though they have to be cleaned before use. I do this by washing the discs in very hot water and washing up liquid, hanging them out to dry, whereupon they can be banged together to knock out all the surplus emulsions. Wear a face mask to avoid inhaling any harmful dusts.
Old green carpet, short tufted type, foam backed and man-made, the tufts being no longer than 9mm. You can very often pick these up from carpet suppliers in samples but beware not to obtain the looped kind.

Paints

Water colours, available from good art shops. W.H. Smith sell these in small palettes at a reasonable price - they tend to be very vibrant in colour but can be toned down in application. I use them all the time.
Acrylics - I find these difficult to use as they dry very quickly, and once applied they cannot be altered, that is, washed out or mixed with other colours on the model. With water colours, on the other hand, the already coloured item can be persuaded to take more colour, changing the tone a little by judicious blending of darker or lighter shades.
Powder Paints - also available from W.H. Smiths and good artists' shops, these come in 'round cardboard tins' and are used for colouring plaster and artex.
Emulsion Paints - handy for colouring foam rubber or latex, adding to water for mixing with artex, and for painting over bare landscape before adding detail.
Varnish - oil based polyurethane, or yacht varnish.
Varnish - water based.
Clear acrylic sheets - Cobex. available from good DIY shops.

In fact, anything, however unlikely, that might seem useful, - give it a try. If it is successful, then all the better; if you fail then you have lost little except time, though you will be richer for the experience...

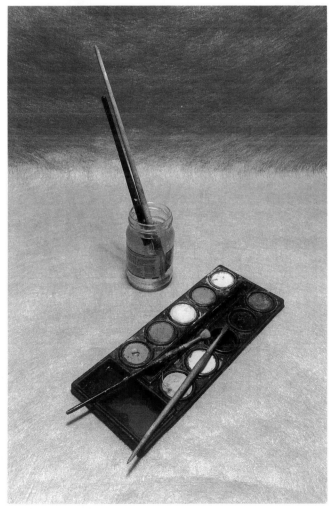

Low cost paint boxes, such as this one, available from W H Smith or Early Learning Centres.

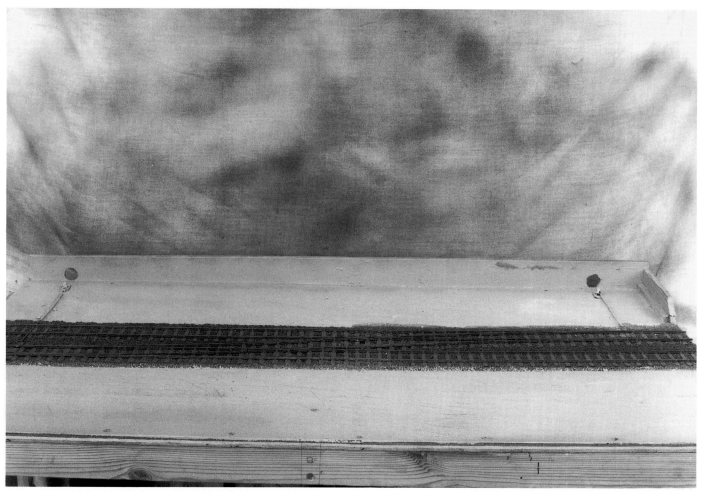

Not the ideal baseboard but very common. (Flat and solid).

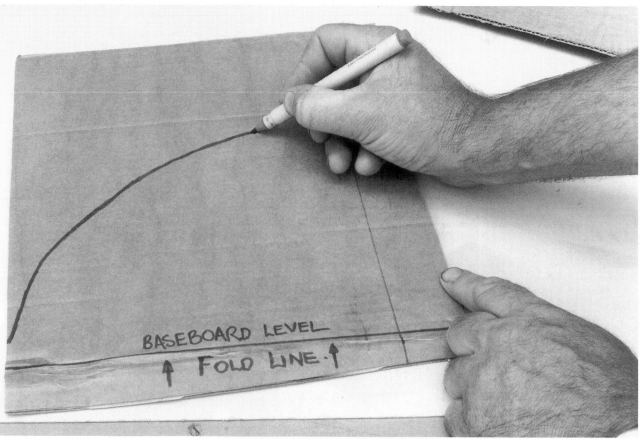

Marking out basic landscape profiles.

Chapter Two
BASIC LANDSCAPING
Building a Foundation for your Landscape, Contouring and Textuing

Whether you are building your landscape on a traditional flat-top baseboard or on an open-frame multi-level structure of some kind, it will be necessary to provide some underlying structure to which the land surface and texturings can be applied. The best way of doing this will be determined by a number of factors, the most important of which will be the sort of landscape you are modelling. Steep, rugged terrain will probably call for a different sort of supporting structure than that required for flat or gently rolling ground.

Before starting out on a landscape foundation, therefore, it is important to decide exactly what sort of result you want to achieve. As mentioned in my introduction, a bit of research and a bit of practical planning to work out the best way of achieving a convincing result, will not come amiss. Remember, in incorporating any cuttings and cliff faces, that the adjoining landscape should be contoured accordingly.

Types of Landscape Sub-Structures
There are two basic forms of landscape modelling - hollow shells of various sorts, and solid laminations of sheet material. Examples of the former include plaster bandage laid over chicken wire, and fabric or paper laid onto a network of card strips; these are often described as 'hard shell' landscaping. 'Solid' systems usually use laminations of lightweight board material, such as expanded polystyrene or compressed wood fibreboard, usually known in the hobby as insulation board. I use both 'hollow' and 'solid' systems of landscape support - a 'hollow' type based on a system of card strips and tissue paper, and a 'solid' alternative, utilising both expanded polystyrene and fibreboard. These are the methods I shall be concentrating on for this book.

'HOLLOW' LANDSCAPE
This technique is based on the use of profiles - pieces of twin-walled corrugated card or plywood, cut to the approximate cross section of the ground being modelled. These are then glued at suitable intervals to provide support for the surface layers, which I make out of woven strips of thin card and PVA glue-impregnated paper towels.

Where hollow landscaping such as this meets the edge of the baseboard, either adjacent to another board, or simply the front or rear edge of the layout, it may be necessary to provide further profiles, usually cut from ply, to both finish off the exposed edge and to provide support for the surfacing along the edge of the structure. Reference to diagrams and photographs should show the bones of this sort of landscape structure.

Where two sections of baseboard carrying built-up landscape meet, it is obviously important that the shape of the terrain on both sides of the join matches up exactly. This is achieved by using pairs of matched profiles, one to finish each separate section of board. Cut them from two sheets of ply at a single go, to make them identical.

Cutting Profiles
Edge profiles or intermediate profiles that need to be structurally strong should be cut from plywood, of say, 6mm thickness. This is best done with a power jigsaw, a very useful tool for layout builders, but if one is not available, thin ply is easy to cut with a fine bladed saw, such as a

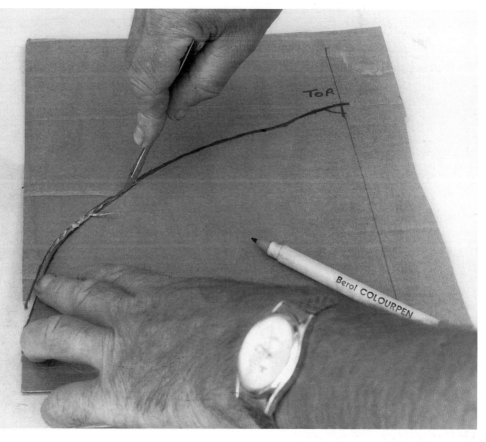

Fingers behind the blade!

Aeons of landscape formation - ice ages, early man, the disappearance of the northern forest - reduced to a few cardboard profiles. It's the sense of power that drives us landscape modellers.

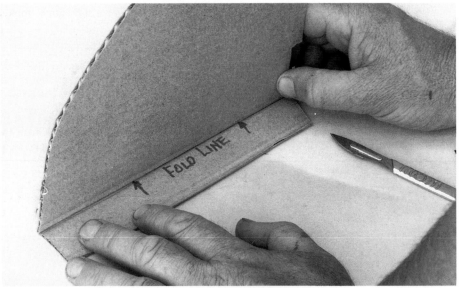

It sounds obvious, but remember to form the profile so that the fold line matches the run of corrugation - imagine trying to fold it the other way.

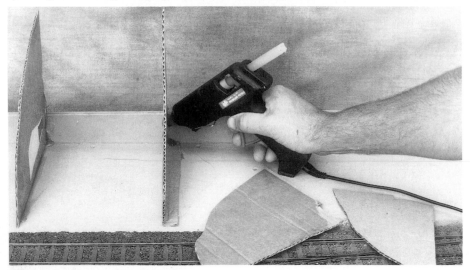

The trusty glue gun fixes it in place.

coping saw, fretsaw or padsaw. You can even purchase a padsaw blade to fit an ordinary Stanley No.199 craft knife handle.

Card profiles can be made out of any suitable thickness of card - I use ordinary double skinned corrugated board, cut from the sort of cartons that supermarket goods come in. Most supermarkets throw these out in huge quantities, and a box that once held 4 dozen tins of baked beans or 40 packets of fancy biscuits will make quite a few landscape profiles. Alternatively, purchase a book mail order from Irwell Press, chuck away the book and use the high quality board wrapping.

When cutting the cardboard, lay it on a firm surface such as an offcut of hardboard; as always, be sure to keep your fingers behind the blade while cutting. I always draw the profiles with a felt tip pen, then cut slight variations in each profile to obtain subtle changes in the 'lie of the land' - again bear your prototype firmly in mind. Either fix the profiles as you go along, or number them so that they are in the right order when you come to fix. I find it best to set the profiles no more than 6-8 inches apart and where there are dramatic changes, such as cuttings with rock faces or cliffs, reduce the gap to 3-4 inches.

Fixing Profiles

The profile pieces are glued to the baseboard structure with the hot glue gun, using either the general purpose glue (clear sticks), or the woodworking glue (white sticks). The glue takes only a few seconds to set off, so you can move swiftly through this process. The ply profiles have enough thickness to make a strong butt joint, but a small section of wood glued to the profile and to the baseboard will give added strength. For the lighter card profiles I find it pays to cut them with enough allowance for a gluing flap to be bent along the bottom edge, as in the photographs.

Surface Support

In the system being described, the actual surface of the landscape is supported by a 'weave' of strips of thin card, cut from cereal packets saved from the dustbin. I make mine about 15mm wide, and cut across the opened out box to give pieces about 18-20 inches long. There is no need for precision in this and the strips can be cut quite roughly, and to differing widths.

The weave is begun by fixing the 'horizontal' strips along the profile pieces, starting at the top/rear of the contours and working back towards the base. The hot glue gun, once again, is the best tool for this job; start at one end profile, and work along the length of the landscape section, tacking the strip to each profile piece as you go. The strips (about three quarters of an inch apart) are simply extended to the required length to span

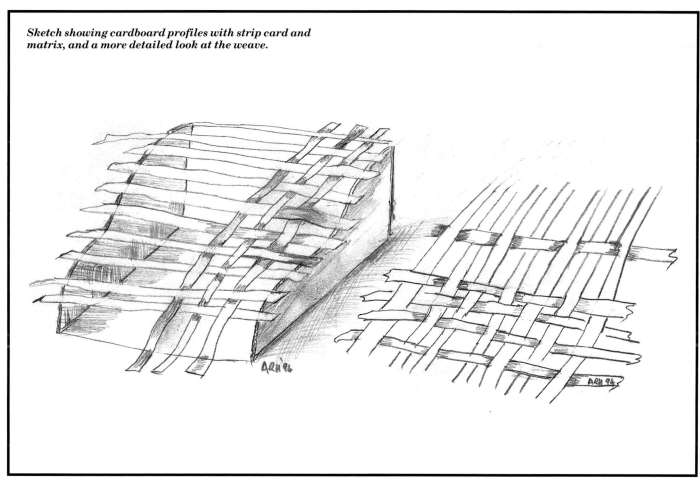

Sketch showing cardboard profiles with strip card and matrix, and a more detailed look at the weave.

the whole section of landscape being modelled, by tacking together with the glue gun, overlapping the joints by about an inch for strength. Make sure that these joints do not cause unwanted humps in the finished surface - joints between profiles are best.

The 'vertical' strips can now be added. These are threaded over and under the horizontal strips, in a simple basket weave fashion, to give a lattice of card. Once again, a gap of around three quarters of an inch is left between adjacent strips. There is no great need to

glue these vertical strips in place as they cannot really go anywhere - the odd tack of hot glue, top and bottom, will be sufficient. I usually insert all my vertical strips working from the centre of a section of horizontals, midway between two profiles, making sure that the

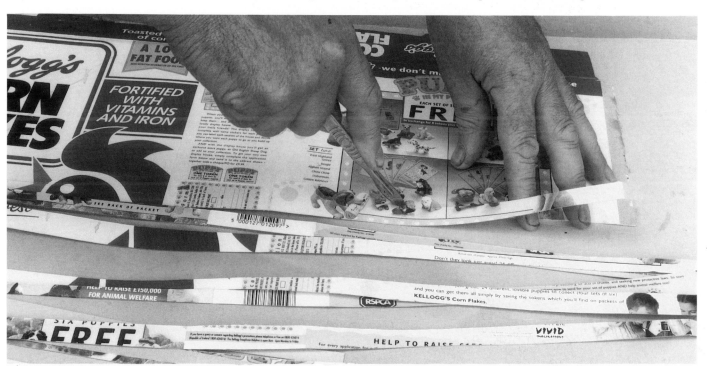

Cutting strips, good **Blue Peter** *stuff.*

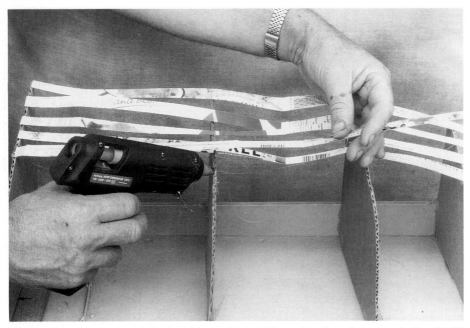

The land surface begins - it looks a bit weak and wilty at first but the strength does build up...

neighbouring strips are woven in opposite ways. That is, if one strip goes over the top horizontal but beneath the next (lower) one, the adjacent strip will go below the top and over the lower one. The vertical strips then can be simply slid out either way to give the required matrix between the profiles. Difficult to describe but easy to do - see the photographs and sketches for clarification.

Chicken Wire
The main alternative to my preferred card matrix support is the more traditional chicken wire, usually in conjunction with an all-plaster surface. This method has been around for many years, but I must say that I have never found it as 'user friendly' as the more modern lightweight systems for creating landscape forms. It seems to me unwieldy, a lot more expensive, and apt to produce very heavy layouts if you are not careful. However, it does have virtue where very large areas of landscape need to be created. I believe many American layouts featuring rugged and mountainous terrain use plaster and chicken wire. These layouts are not very portable! Nevertheless there are many people who do favour this system, even

for British style portable layouts, so I feel it must rate a mention here. As with the card matrix, the wire surface support is carried on profiles, but due to the weight and the relative stiffness of the wire mesh, these will all need to be cut from ply of a reasonable thickness, say 6mm or more. These are glued, screwed or nailed firmly in place on the baseboard structure. The wire is then attached to the profiles with staples, either fired from a heavy duty staple gun, or hammered in. The whole process is a great deal slower and less adaptable than the card structures.

The Surface
Having constructed our supporting matrix of card or chicken wire, it is now necessary to cover it with a suitable material for the actual surface, to which the texturing and detailing will be applied. There are a number of alternatives at this stage, of which plaster-impregnated scrim bandage or some form of papier mache are the most popular. I combine the two, using a rather stronger form of papier mache than the usual wallpaper paste and newspaper type, made of paper hand towels fixed with PVA glue, which are then coated with a coloured texturing plaster mix.

The paper for this process needs to have reasonable wet strength, otherwise it will tend to disintegrate when the plaster slurry is applied, hence my preference for towels. The sort of coarse stuff that garage forecourts (sometimes) provide is ideal, and can be bought in large rolls from the better motor factors and some DIY motor stores. Useful and easily obtained alternatives are the familiar green Cresco

...once the weave gets underway.

Those awful green folded towels found in less salubrious conveniences. It will not do your Rotary Club standing any good at all to be caught 'gathering them'.

'Convenience modelling' you could call this.

The glue goes on...

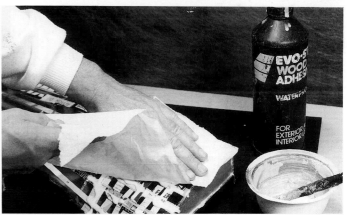

...our previously obtained towelling is pressed on top...

...to give this sort of result. We now have the bare bones of a landscape.

folded paper towels found in your average convenience. They can of course be obtained furtively but be aware of the social consequences of being apprehended... The plastermix is made from decorative texturing ceiling plaster, the stuff generally known as Artex, a trade name that, like Hoover, has come to cover the whole range of similar products. This can be bought in modest packets from DIY stores such as Great Mills or B & Q, or in larger bags from Builders' Merchants

Applying the Surfacing

The basic paper towel or strong tissue is glued to the card matrix with neat PVA glue - spread generously over the card strips with a large paintbrush. The paper is then laid gently over the glued matrix, and pressed carefully into the glue. If required, a second or subsequent layer of tissue can be added, by brushing a coat of PVA glue (thinned down) carefully over the first layer of tissue, repeating the process. All this work must be done whilst the glue on the first layer is still wet.

With the glued tissue skin in place on the matrix, the next layer of surface, the plastermix, can be applied. With a reasonable size of decorator's paintbrush (about an inch), spread the creamy plaster over the tissue, gently stippling as you

Step by step 1-9 with the Artex and PVA, achieving the right colour by a 'dry shake' in the chosen container.

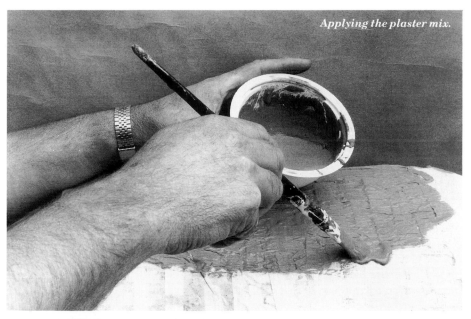

Applying the plaster mix.

with the heat, though; if it is too fierce then the plaster may crack as it dries. Once it is properly dry, the result is a base shell for the landscaping which is reasonably strong, and to which textures and detailing can be added.

Mixing and Colouring Plaster

To prevent white plaster showing through landscape textures and finishes (minor chips are inevitable) the plastermix is pre-coloured in a suitable shade of grey or brown, depending on the landscape type, rocks and soil being modelled. A suitable agent is needed and I use either ordinary matt emulsion paints, or powder colour. These 'colorants' have to be used in different ways, as follows-

Emulsion paint is mixed with water to which a drop of washing up liquid has been added, to reduce the surface tension;

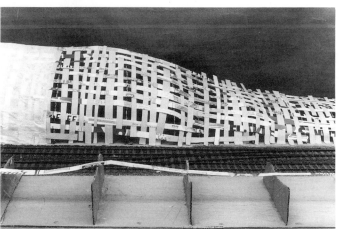

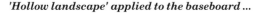

'Hollow landscape' applied to the baseboard ...

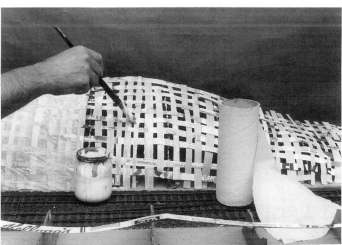

... and that towelling again ...

this mix is then blended with PVA glue to about the consistency of semi-skimmed milk, and this in turn is added to the Artex powder, to give a final result about as thick as double cream. The colouring of the plastermix thus obtained is less consistent than the method described in the next paragraph, and slightly varying shades will occur when the plaster is dry.

Second option: powder colour is mixed 'dry' with the Artex powder. I do this by placing a quantity of Artex - usually about a standard baked bean can full - in a clear plastic bag or screwlid plastic container, such as a plastic sweet jar. The powder colour is then added and blended until the right colour is achieved in this dry mix, by shaking the chosen container vigorously. I have found that the colour of such a dry mix is more or less the colour the finished plaster will eventually dry to, once laid. The powder paint/artex mix is then further mixed, with PVA glue and water, the latter in a ratio of 25% PVA glue to 75% water (approximately). Continuing my culinary analogy, the plastermix should now have a consistency of double cream.

go. If the tissue should tear all is not lost; extra pieces can be laid into the plaster, which will be bonded into place for a permanent repair. Be careful to treat the edges of any such patches carefully and to bed them down properly, disguising the joints. You may also find that the tissue rucks up and forms wrinkles - do not be

troubled by this, for it simply adds more texture to the landscape surface.

The completed and surfaced landscaping should now be left to dry. This usually takes between 12 and 24 hours at normal room temperatures, but you may be able to hurry matters along with the careful use of a hairdryer. Go easy

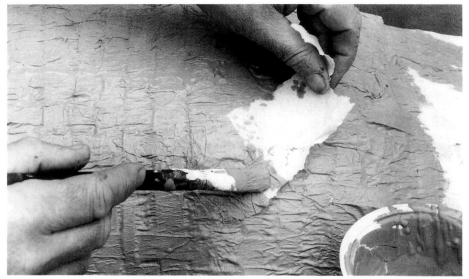

If a tear occurs all is not lost. A carefully laid tissue patch is all that is required.

'SOLID' LANDSCAPE

The main alternative to building up landscape from formers and surface skins is to carve it from the solid. The basic approach is to build up a suitable bulk to carve from, and this can be achieved by laminating together several layers of an appropriate material. The main use is where very large areas of raised landscape are needed, which would be very slow to build up from card matrix hardshell. Laminated solid landscaping can also be

Laminated landscaping ...

... with plastermix applied.

very good at replicating certain types of terrain, such as stratified rock cuttings or cliffs. I make considerable use of laminated landscaping, either on its own or combined with the hard-shell techniques. The materials I use for laminations are, as already mentioned, fibreboard and expanded polystyrene. The techniques for wrestling these materials into some sort of order differ considerably...

Laminated Fibreboard Landscaping

Let's consider fibreboard (compressed wood fibre insulating board, to give it its full title) first. It usually comes in 8ft x 4ft sheets about five eighths of an inch thick, with one finished face in white or ivory. A common trade name is 'Tentest Board' and builders' merchants, timber yards and some DIY outlets can supply it. It is, moreover, relatively cheap.

The board is easily fashioned and can be cut with a knife or saw, or simply broken apart with the fingers. The layers are stuck to the base and each other with PVA glue or the hot glue gun, with a few panel pins for good measure. The edge of each layer is set back slightly from the one below to form a 'step contour'; the degree to which each layer is set back determines the slope of the finished ground.

The joined laminae can be carved with a knife or saw, or the final contours arrived at by filling the 'steps' with a papier mache made of torn up tissue or newsprint, soaked in dilute PVA. Smooth this into the contours and over the surface of the board and leave to dry, preferably in a warm room. Try not to get the insulation board too wet as water (squeeze excess fluid from the papier mache) can cause it to break down and become soft and pulpy. Where steep rocky faces are needed, this material and method can be very useful. By breaking off small pieces and stacking them steeply, perhaps with a card or wood backing, you can build up vertical or near-vertical surfaces with a pleasing 'stratified' surface that can be coated with plastermix to make a convincing rockface; more on this in the section on 'rockwork'.

The drawback to laminated fibreboard landscaping is that, in large amounts, it can become surprisingly heavy. If you are not careful, you can end up with baseboards that take a double hernia heave to move!

Laminated Polystyrene Landscaping

For large areas of laminated landscape, something lighter is needed as a basic material, and expanded polystyrene is ideal. There are three main sources for this: ceiling tiles, around half an inch thick, widely available from DIY outlets and very cheap; wall or floor insulation, a rather denser grade of polystyrene from 1-6 inches thick, sold in slabs about 4ft x

Using insulation board as a layering can create a more gentle, time-worn look to the rock faces - for an almost perfect illustration of the 'stepped' effect, see the formation above the line on page 10, top.

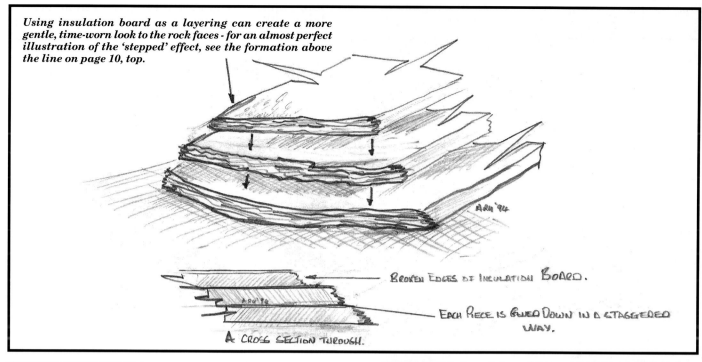

BROKEN EDGES OF INSULATION BOARD.

EACH PIECE IS GLUED DOWN IN A STAGGERED WAY.

A CROSS SECTION THROUGH.

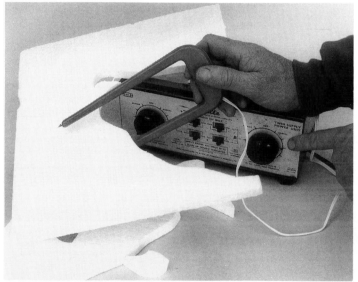

Cutting polystyrene.

Polystyrene packages from some electrical equipment.

Ceiling tiles ...

... wrestled into desired shape.

Rudimentary stepping.

16 inches (or in 8ft x 4ft sheets) at builders' merchants, usually under the trade name 'Jablite' and thirdly, in irregular - but often very useful - chunks from discarded packing supplied with domestic appliances, hi-fi, TVs and so on. A friendly electrical shop may well be persuaded to give you this sort of stuff.

The main drawback to expanded polystyrene as a landscaping material is the mess you make cutting and carving it. It can easily be cut with a hacksaw blade, serrated kitchen knife or similar implement, but the little beads of polystyrene released by the process will follow you everywhere; even the most

powerful vacuum cleaner won't deter the little perishers from entering any and every crevice, and then staying there. This can result in domestic friction...

There is a tool, supplied by Proops Educational Packages, which is shaped like a magnet and has a replaceable element, stretched across its open end,

Glueing tiles together with plastermix.

Adding plastermix to our steps.

which when heated will cut polystyrene neatly and cleanly. To use it, you need to connect two wires to the 12 volt DC outlets on your locomotive controller - by depressing the button on the styrene cutter, an electrical current is allowed to heat the element. Be careful that you do not have the controller turned up too high, as the element will very quickly burn out. (see photographs).

Gluing this polystyrene in place or laminating it is quite tricky, for it is impossible to use a petroleum-based adhesive - this will chomp into the stuff as if it has not had a good meal for weeks. Unfortunately most of the contact types - Evo-stik, UHU, Bostik and so on, are petroleum based. A special adhesive for the job - EPA, or Expanded Polystyrene Adhesive - is available, but expensive. I have found that for modelling purposes a mixture of PVA glue and Artex, at about the consistency of thick mud, will do the job. While this is setting off, it is a good idea to have a few weights to hold everything in place.

Once the laminae are in place, they can be treated and surfaced with either the papier mache or tissue and plastermix, as already described; the plaster impregnated bandages (Modroc and the rest) are also good as a surface for laminated polystyrene landscaping.

Beauty is Skin Deep

With the landscape foundations and the basic surface complete and dry, we are ready to move on to the really interesting part of the basic landscape modelling process - adding the surface texture and vegetation....

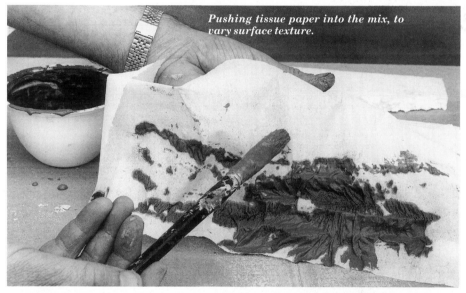

Pushing tissue paper into the mix, to vary surface texture.

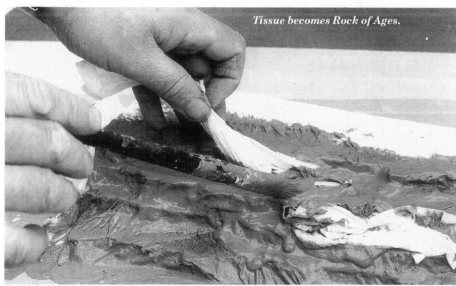

Tissue becomes Rock of Ages.

Stratified rock need not always form the grandiose setting - a discrete outcrop, largely obscured like this, can be terribly effective, draped in vegetation.

This mix of rock, walling and hewn stone will add to the realism of any railway model. Photograph D. Ibbotson.

Chapter Three
ON THE ROCKS

When the Engineers built our railway system, they inevitably came upon the need to carve through hillsides, creating in the process (amongst many other things) rock faced cuttings. Recreating these rock cuttings in model form has always given me great pleasure. It is a fairly straightforward process and by following my step by step methods, I hope that you too will derive as much pleasure from your own rocks and rock faces. Before embarking on this stage of the modelling, I would strongly advise some research into the type of rock that is prevalent to your chosen region - is it limestone, granite, sandstone, or something else?

Forming a rock face
I form a vertical or near-vertical face with either a good quality card or thin plywood, which is then fixed using the hot glue gun, tacking the bottom edge to the baseboard or trackbed. This is then strengthened by pieces of card or plywood, glued at right angles to the back. Once I am happy with this I proceed to coat the plywood/card, a small area at a time, with neat PVA glue, having first of all mixed my chosen colour of plastermix for the desired landscape surface - as described in the previous chapter. I like to make this mix fairly thick, and add a little PVA glue for extra adhesive strength.

Taking a palette knife, I proceed to coat the glued area with a thick layer of plaster. I let this dry slowly, working it all the time with the palette knife, creating fissures and strata as I go. As this is the first coat I tend not to worry too much about detail - at this stage we are concerned more with the basic shapes. Once content, I move on to the next area and repeat the process until I have reached the end of the rock face. By this time the first coat on the first section should be nearly dry, I then add more plaster and start putting in the real detail, using the palette knife and small paintbrush. I find that as more plaster coats are applied and dry, the next coat will dry quicker than the last, so I need to work fairly swiftly towards the end of the process. When a fairly thick coat has been built up, jutting rocks can be added by pushing the plaster down and drawing it out, in the same manner as the old butter patters used to do on slabs of marble in Sainsbury's, for those of us who can remember. The photographs and sketches will give a clearer picture.

Rock
Where I need to form outcrops of rock on a landscape, I take tissue paper, screw it up, soak it in PVA glue and water to form a papier mache, and stick this down wherever it's needed, giving it a coat of thin plastermix of the consistency used to create the adjacent landscape surface, as mentioned in the previous chapter. Once this has dried I proceed with a thicker plastermix, as used in creating rock faces, trowelled on with a palette knife and worked in a similar manner as described previously. Again photographs and sketches will make this clearer.

Dove Hole Tunnel and Jubilee 4-6-0 45553 CANADA - the 'stepped' effect once more is apparent, on both sides of the cutting. It is quite usual for such cuttings, from the craggy limestone of the Pennines to the chalk of the Yorkshire and Dorset coasts, to be assymetrical in their cross sections - that is, the sides will have different angles of slope. This is often due to the 'lay' of the strata - because the rock layers dip from one side to another (they are often not wholly horizontal) the layers on the 'up' slope are less stable. Many such cuttings degraded over the years and brickwork/stonework is added to secure dangerous bits. The point is, don't be afraid to make a cutting that is not a 'mirror image' one side to the other. The reality was often far from that. Photograph E.R. Morten.

The plastermix before being applied, showing consistency.

Apply PVA glue (left) followed by the first coat (bottom) of pre-coloured plaster mix.

This page: trowelling in the strata, progressively working the layers and fissures to give a 'mature' rockface .

Break up the horizontal layering with vertical features.

The 'trend' of rock can run through 90 degrees, from horizontal to vertical, so don't be afraid of any 'angle'. The further north and west you go in Britain, the less likely it is you find horizontal strata.

Doing the work of ages - 'weathering' of rock really is that - wind, rain and temperature action. A trowel is quicker.

Derbyshire limestone it ain't - the heather alone reveals that - this rock has been tilted so that its 'layers' are nearly vertical rather than horizontal, a sharp contrast to The Peak. Shoved up like this, the rock is exposed to ice and wind, giving this 'sharpened' appearance. Photograph Peter Barnfield

A rocky outcrop built up on tissue paper, then plastered.

Applying water colour paints. Don't carry on horizontal strata for too long - interrupt with vertical zones, knock them about a bit, as here. As nature, avoid neatness.

Painting

I find water colours a particular good medium for rock, as I can flood the whole outcrop, building up individual areas with various shades to create the illusion of weathered rock. Where cracks and fissures have been formed, then the water will be drawn into them, highlighting the natural faults and layers. Where the rock face projects I plant tufts of grass as described in the following chapter. In the shadow of the projection I like to add darker colours, just to highlight this detail.

Water seeping through a rock face is an attractive feature, portrayed by painting the model carefully with gloss varnish. If there are any trees or shrubs close to the edge of the face, a further natural detail might well be an exposed root system. This is particularly common in chalk and sandstone areas. I portray this by painting a bead of hot glue which I have applied to the top edge of the cliff face and pulling the glue off to form a string, which is attached to the plaster.

Limestone again and Monsal Dale again, in The Peak, a good example of a stratified rock face - bare, because of its steepness. Such rocks are largely confined to the east side of England, though they outcrop from Yorkshire to the south coast. In this country the layers are horizontal or gently sloping, a reflection of their relative youthfulness.

Chapter Four
AT THE GRASS ROOTS

Much has been written of the various methods for replicating grass on layouts but I propose in this chapter to cover only those I have found to work well. These methods require the use of hairy carpet underfelt, lint and latex scatter materials.

Let there be Light - and Colour

When starting to grass over a given area of textured landscape, remember that, though it seems obvious, colour plays an enormous part in the final 'look'. It is a worthwhile exercise to check that your colouring is right, I find; a quick consultation with my wife (you'll have to find your own) usually proves highly beneficial, as (apparently) men are more likely to be colour blind than women.

We must bear colours particularly in mind when working under artificial lighting, for certain fluorescent lights will enhance greens and blues. I have seen some pretty glowing green layouts on the exhibition circuit, where I am sure the modeller has built the layout in one light and is exhibiting it under another, harsher kind. In recent years there has been much research into fluorescent lighting and innovations by firms such as Philips have brought a fluorescent tube

The Peak again, though only layouts devoted to North America seem prepared to tackle this sort of scene. The Brits with our little branch lines tend to quail at the prospect. Stick a trestle in and the obligatory box car or loco half buried in the stream bed and this could be the Little Susquehanna and Alberqurque or something equally bizarre.

The variety in grass lengths here are obvious and with careful attention can be created in model form. And that wall!

Ancient Caledonia.

Silver Birch in open country.

Added details such as dead and fallen trees are seldom modelled but are common in real life.

Engineers and Mother Nature in harmony albeit in model form.

This stone wall was built using small balls of Das.

Marginal plants with varying colours add greatly to the overall effect. Note in 'cutaway' use of Cobex - bottom right - to create illusion of depth.

Rock cuttings with overhanging plants can give pleasure before, during and after their creation.

Moving water.

Erosion has exposed the roots of this tree.

The tree to the right requires its foliage.

that reduces flicker, and gives a better light. This particular tube is a TBL slimline type and a 4ft 36w/35 fluorescent tube, I am led to believe, will suit modellers. I should add that this lighting tube is used for shop displays.

Commercially available scatter material is useful for portraying grass, leaves and so on and is a coloured, crushed latex. Suppliers include Set Scenes, Carrs and Greenscene - addresses at the end. When purchasing scatter material at exhibitions, remember it is being displayed under often dubious artificial lighting conditions, which, as we have seen, will make the colours seem brighter, so it is probably better to go for the duller shades of the range - unless of course you are modelling spring, with lots of yellow/orange/brown or autumn, when yellowy greens, reds and plenty of mellow fruitfulness will abound.

Time for Planting
Area and railway company chosen, start looking at the countryside. To my mind this is the next best thing to heaven, and transferring the contours of the real world, with all its vegetation, into model form, is a very rewarding part of our hobby. Note where trees stand, and where the fences run, what hedges are around, whether there are any walls nearby, how long is the grass? Are we depicting summer, autumn or spring? - all very

The subtleties of grass. The best modelled stuff is hardly noticeable.

important pointers for capturing that natural feel.

Embankments
Take a railway embankment, for example; in the early years of the railway era these would be devoid of trees, so lots of grass would be the order of the day, and in some places it would very short, especially after

a visit from the lengthmen, whose job it was to keep the lineside tidy and avoid fires from the flying coals of locomotives.

With time, nature takes its grip, and gorse, brambles, small shrubby trees, nettle beds and of course rosebay willow herb will all have taken hold, adding more character to an otherwise relatively bare embankment. Lupins, of all things, once

Tufts of grass nestle on the many ledges alongside small shrubs etc. Photograph H.C. Casserley.

Underfelt. Strictly traditional cutting method.

characterised the Kings Cross approaches - so effectively, anything goes in the scrub stakes. This is 'climax vegetation' - that is, the maturing urge, from grass ultimately to forest - in progress. The natural process was ever kept in check by maintenance, but abandonment of such attention by BR in recent years makes for dense scrub, bushes and young trees now on many former grass slopes.

Modern motorway embankments often provide good examples of what I am describing. If we look at a newly opened motorway, and then look at it again in two - three years, the difference in the vegetation will be enormous. The cutting through the chalk escarpment at the southern end of the M40 is a famous example - its bare rock of a few year ago is weathered and well on the way to a carpet of green. If you are modelling in 4mm or 7mm to the foot, the following methods are applicable, but I feel they might have limited use in 2mm scale.

Hairy Grass
I have found that certain carpet underlays have a tendency to look like dead grass - when treated, paradoxically, with tender loving care. I am talking of the self-coloured natural hairy fibre type of carpet underlay, which is a light beige colour. It can be purchased from good carpet shops or, if you are having problems obtaining it from such outlets, then Set Scenes of Crawley will be able to supply your needs.

There are other colours of carpet felt underlay, dark blue for instance, a grey one and a brown one, the brown being more hairy than the other two; they are made, I believe, of cotton waste, rendering them unsuitable for our needs. With an abundance of dark brown hairy underfelt available, the need to bleach this material makes it (for me) unsuitable - I tend, therefore, to steer clear of the methods described in recent years for using this form of underlay.

Taking the natural light coloured underfelt as a good base for grass, it can be treated in two distinctly different ways:

Grass Matting
This method is a good way of covering large areas very quickly. Before proceeding, make sure your work area is well ventilated, as the Copydex glue is quite obnoxious.

The Big Rip Off. One surface of the underfelt is coated in Copydex and when dry 'delaminated' from main sheet.

... giving a strong, flexible grass map.

Grass tufts.

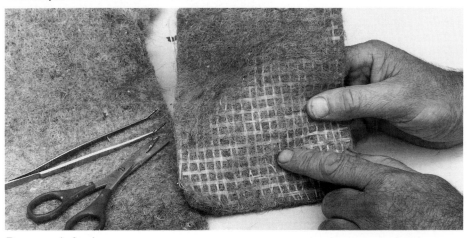

Remove reinforcing.

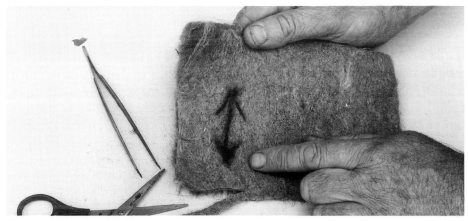

Check the 'grain' (see text).

Cut into strips.

Cut a piece of underfelt, say about 18ins by 9ins, and lay this on a flat surface covered with newspaper. Apply a thick coat of Copydex glue to the uppermost surface, stippling into the hairy felt as you progress across the sheet. Allow this to dry, then apply one more coat, working this into the first coat as previously described. Set to one side and allow to dry thoroughly. Once dry, pick up the underfelt and, carefully working from one corner, begin to 'unlaminate' the felt. As you proceed carefully across the piece you will notice that you are beginning to form a matting, or turf, of grass. When you have completed 'unlaminating' the sheet, this turf will be found to be very flexible and strong, allowing it to be glued in any location on your embankment. If you have any projecting rocks, or rock faces, then all you need to do here is to cut a hole approximately the shape of the projection. Spread glue over the textured surface - I tend to favour Resin W, but Copydex will do - and simply press the turf into the glue, leaving to dry. Once dry you can trim any surplus overhanging pieces with either a sharp knife, or a pair of scissors. Any gaps that you may have around projecting rocks and rockfaces can be treated with tufts of grass, described in the next section.

Grass Tufts

This method is more laborious than the previous one, but gives a better representation - I find there is more control over the density and length of the grass.

Taking a piece of underfelt, cut it to approximately 6ins square and 'unlaminate' into approximately half its original thickness. You will probably find in the middle of this sheet a reinforcing matrix, made of string, nylon thread or strips of polythene bonded into squares - remove this as it will only make for problems later on. Now take the reduced thickness and check the way the fibres run - up or down, or across. Take a pair of sharp scissors and cut across the grain, so as to gain short strands or fibres. You will form strips from approximately quarter of an inch to three eighths of an inch wide. This really depends on the chosen scale but generally anywhere within these sizes will give a good effect. This sounds a little complicated but a close study of the photographs will, I hope, make matters plain. Cut a goodly few of these strips and set to one side. Now spread neat Resin W (water resistant glue) over an area approximately three inches square. The glue should be reasonably thick, to allow us to plant the tufts of fibre. Take a strip and press one end into the glue, holding that end in the glue with your pair of tweezers (an old electrical screwdriver will do) and pull the remaining strip away, leaving a large tuft in the glue. Proceed in the same manner

Here the glue is being applied followed (right)by the grass tufts.

all the way along the edge of the glue in the horizontal plane, and work your way up the glue in the same way, thus covering the whole area with little tufts of fibres. Working in this way you will quickly cover a large area with varying lengths of grass; if time presses, do not worry about leaving a portion 'ungrassed' overnight - come back to it the next day and the joins will blend together, almost indistinguishably.

Using this method you can plant grass almost anywhere, where it will grow naturally in the real world, i.e. between rails, edges of paths and roadways, around the foundations of railway buildings and so on. Leave all the grass so treated to dry for at least twelve hours in a warm room, before you attempt to colour it.

Colouring the Grass
Water colours lend themselves best for this (acrylics I find tend to dry to a hard and 'crispy' finish) and by using lots of water, the hairy fibres take in the paint pigments at varying rates. Subtle changes in shades thus appear as the paint dries.

Tufts of 'grass' (above and below) planted in rock crevices.

Load a No.7 or larger paint brush (or something similar) with water and paint; begin with a dark green and wash over the whole area, dabbing in other colours, from yellow through to blues, greens, browns and even white. All these are generously diluted and if working on a cutting, be careful not to allow too much water to drain onto the trackbed Once this mess has dried, take somrthing like a suede brush and tease up the fibres - it is then that the full effect of the colouring process can be seen. If unhappy with the result, then it's a simple matter to add extra colour as needed. I find that in most cases the fibres will be too long, so I snip them back to the required length with a pair of scissors.

The suede brush will have plenty of fibres caught up in the bristles - careful extraction frees these for recycling on the embankment/cutting/slope whatever. I lay them over the chosen area, thinning slightly as I go (a wide variety of ground cover can be achieved - nettles or

The typical branch embankment - grass, herbs, thistle, gorse, blackthorn - managed waste ground, in effect.

whatever) and gently apply hairspray and add a pinch or two of scatter, dropped like light rain from a height of say 18 inches. The hairspray will act as a fixative for most of the scatter and will keep the 'hairy' grass standing in its final, 'real' position.

Lint
Although lint has been advocated as a very good material for portraying grass, I have found it of limited efficacy in the larger scales. It is simply stuck down and

then pulled off and I tend to use it in sheet form, preferring to work from the solid as it were, rather than in tufts, which is the usual method of application.

I start by sticking down a sheet over the chosen area using PVA water resistant glue, making sure the hairy side is uppermost, smoothing the sheet out to remove all the creases and air bubbles, then leaving to dry. I then wash the whole area in water colours, in the fashion detailed above; drying time is dependent on temperature, but once dry a suede

brush serves to bring up the fibres. Scatter materials are added to make a variety of ground cover and changes in the surface, making for more of that wonder ingredient, realism.

Scatter
Scatter is particulate latex, and handy stuff indeed. It is widely used in the hobby and is also described in the chapter dealing with trees, but a few notes here will be useful too.

Scatter is graded from fine to coarse, which means a pleasing variety of textures can be achieved in the smaller scales, but I feel it is best used in tandem with other materials, such as hairy underfelt, to give a really good representation of vegetation when modelling in 4mm and above. When using the stuff on its own, without lint or underfelt, use emulsion paint, PVA glue or hairspray as an adhesive. There is also - though I warn, they can be excessively smelly and expensive - spray adhesives available from the print world and carpet fitting trade. Be aware that these will almost certainly need extraction arrangements, or a spray mask at the least.

Using PVA glue or emulsion paint, liberally coat the ground to be grassed, then sprinkle with varying shades and grades of scatter; with a paper towel press gently and bed the granules/ particles down, then leave to dry in a warm room. Dust off and collect any remaining loose particles, which can then be recycled. Small tufts of carpet or hairy felt can be added, often to very good effect - see photographs.

Don't forget the seaside - MONA and MANNIN head the 4pm from Douglas on June 26th 1961. The trees will be low, stunted and fashioned and shaped by the prevailing wind. Photograph P.J. Lynch.

Note bark and 'nobbly bits'.

Old oak in pasture land. Note the 'flat bottom' so characteristic of trees in farmland - a result of grazing.

Ivy always makes a tree in model form more interesting.

Bark and suckers.

Chapter Five
GROWING YOUR OWN TREES

What can be done. Plastic Oak after surgery.

Sowing the Seeds

In scenic modelling, it is observation that bears the most fruit. This is straining the horticultural imagery a bit, but to model trees successfully it is a must, as a first step, to get amongst the trees and feel their majesty. I understand we cannot all go tramping off to the woods in the New Age way, but most parks and open spaces within towns will have quite a few mature native trees, as indeed will quite a few of our streets. It is always worthwhile to take a look at these (be they big or small) throughout the year - winter, summer, autumn and spring. Even a few snapshots at the relevant times will serve you well when you come to start to model your trees. When photographing or looking at trees a small pocket book for identifying the species is most useful.

As I mentioned in the introduction, there are trees that will grow almost anywhere and those that are very regional in their distribution, so be very careful when setting out to model a particular species - make sure that they are found growing in the areas where your railway is based.

It is probably a very good idea, if this is your first attempt at building trees, to start with a small specimen, say a hawthorn - they are prolific, abundant, and appear in most parts of the countryside, most commonly in hedgerows.

Methods in use Today

There are, to my knowledge, seven ways to come up with trees, four of them involving the use of wire of some description. There are two plastic types, susceptible of alteration and adaptation, and there is also a 'natural way'. This book is mainly concerned with the 'unnatural' methods, but to be fair to Mother Nature a paragraph on the 'natural' way follows...

Au Naturel

I always feel that twigs and such like material, flowerheads and so on, will always look like - twigs and flowerheads, no matter what is done to them. Heather, privet hedging (small box privet), yarrow heads, hydrangea heads, twigs from various trees and bushes and doubtless many more have all been tried, including in recent times some dried plants from South Africa. These latter immigrants, to be fair, have a good shape, and probably represent the best 'plants as trees' imitations available. Apart from this African exotic, I have tried all the 'prototypes' mentioned above, and a few more - all (to my mind) have failed to convincingly impersonate a tree, for it is difficult to alter the shape and size and, essentially, that difficult to define scale, that nature has given to a plant.

Plastic Trees

These have been around for many years, going back to the pre-dawn of modelling, and one make, Britain's Trees, appear in photographs of railway layouts in scales ranging from HO to O gauge. There have been oaks, cedars and pines, along with poplars and firs from Merit Trees, all with plug-in branches and foliage. They were very good for their day, but always looked the same, and you could spot them a mile

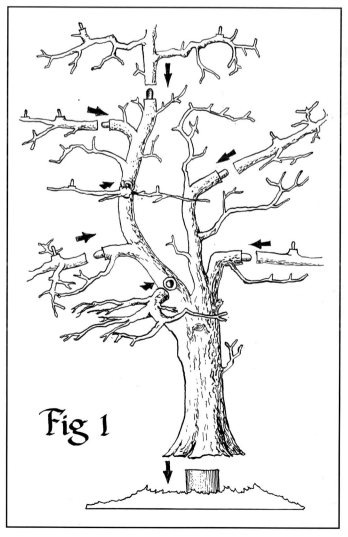

Fig 1

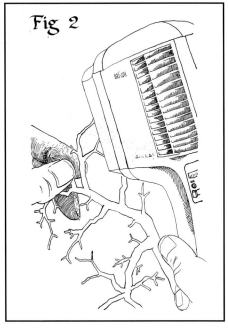

Fig 2

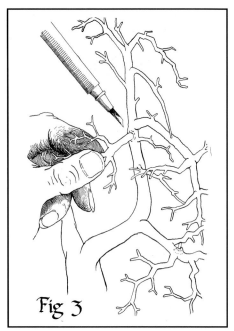

Fig 3

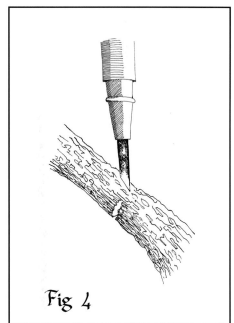

Fig 4

Fig 5

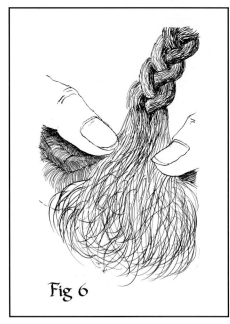

Fig 6

Fig 7

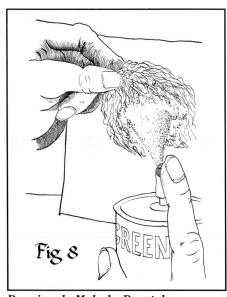

Fig 8

Drawings by Malcolm Dunstal.

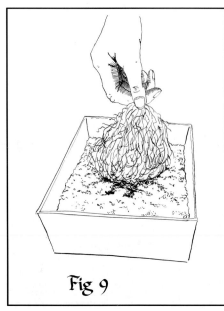

Fig 9

Fig 10

off, on any of the layouts featured in such 1960s magazines as Railway Modeller, Model Railway News and Model Railway Constructor. Just a thumb through these worthy journals will yield many examples.

To alter these plastic trees, which I believe are still available in toy shops, you will need an old soldering iron, hairdryer, enamel or acrylic paints, spray paint from a car accessory shop, a sharp knife and plenty of ventilation. Foliage is dealt with elsewhere in this chapter. The sketches will show you how I have altered them, but to start with, plug all the branches into the trunk. Take a hairdryer and warm the small branches until they become pliable, then bend them to the desired position. Taking this one step further, carefully cut off a branch or two and with the soldering iron, weld the branch onto another part of the trunk, gently stroking the soldering iron tip down the plastic, to form a bark effect. To ring the changes even further, take the hot soldering iron again, push it into the trunk and drag it slowly down the front of the tree to form a split, thus emulating a lightening strike, tidying up the bark by gently stroking the bulging molten plastic. Any further scars can be done in a similar way but do all this work in very well ventilated conditions. For holes, just push in the hot iron and draw it out slowly and finish as mentioned above.

Spray the tree with a grey primer, leave to dry in a warm room, or gently play the warm air from the hairdryer to speed up the drying process. Once dry you can proceed to paint the specimen trees with various shades of grey, greens and blacks and - not so much - brown. Using a sable hair paintbrush No.7, work the green and black into the fissures of the bark, blending as you go, and then dry brush over the top to show up nature's imperfections. Within a short while the tree will start to look less like a plastic tree, and more like the real thing in miniature. Leaves are dealt with in the following sections.

Forestry the Set Scenes way.

Modern Plastic Trees

There are many types of trees produced by continental model makers such as Heki: I have little knowledge of these but have had some experience with the kits produced by Set Scenes. They are primarily one species, Scots Pine, though they are perhaps more versatile in that they can be altered in shape as you build them. Once again the principle of construction is plug and socket, glued together using a plastic weld type of adhesive.

Once you have constructed these trees following the maker's instructions, painting them using acrylic paints and enamels is simple. They are a quick and very useful answer for small copses in the middle to far distance, on any size layout, in scales from 2 - 4mm to the foot.

The Wire Tree.

Copper wire from all manner of sources can be employed - 30 amp cooker wire, old imperial 13 amp ring main wire (multi-stranded and usually in a grey

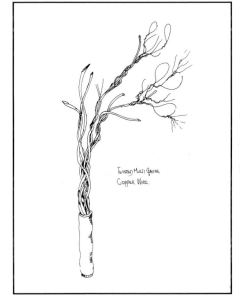

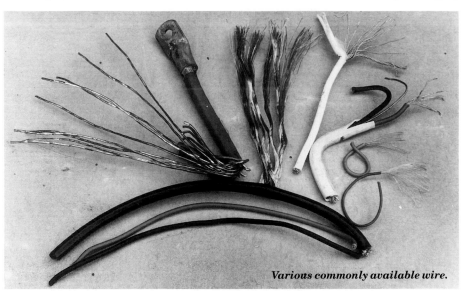

Various commonly available wire.

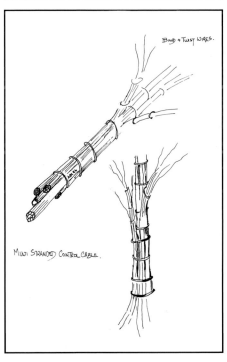

plastic sheathing, with the old black, red and green colour coding) earth cable (metric) which is shrouded with green and yellow striped plastic, multi-stranded lighting flex, 'tails' - used to connect domestic fuse boards - industrial cable used in trunking; in fact, most wire in almost any gauge.

'Control' Wire

Much has been written about constructing trees from control wire, of which it would seem there are many variations - I will deal with the one I know best. You'll need several lengths of 7 x 7 cable (the lengths of course depend on the scale in which you are modelling). The 7 denotes that there are 7 wires to each of 7 strands which go to make up the whole - 49 wires in all. 'Control' wire, also known as 'Bowden' cable, is a springy steel wire available from good hardware shops and ships chandlers, etc. Avoid stainless steel wire, which expensive and of no use.

To minimise damage to fingers it is best to soften the wire, by heating it to a bright red colour, then leaving it to cool slowly - the slower the better. It is not possible to solder up the wires once they have been annealed, and bear in mind that the wire will rust rapidly once it has been heated. Taking the bunch of softened wires, bind them together with single strands approximately 15mm apart to form the main trunk. Where a branch breaks away, separate several strands and twist these together, binding the break with another single strand of wire. Work on up the tree, forming the main branches as you go. Each main bough is then treated as the trunk, and wires are twisted out in a bifurcating progress, working the separate various strands to form smaller branches, and then eventually the smallest branches. When this has been completed, take a hot glue gun and proceed to tack and coat all the main branches and trunk of the tree, making sure that all the wires are covered, except where the smallest extremities - we can call them 'twigs' - have been formed. These are treated differently - see later, 'Forming a Bark'.

Copper Wire Methods - Fine Multi Stranded Cable

This way of doing things requires more patience but many fine models have been produced in this material. Strip the outer cable insulation off to expose the copper wire and, using a few strands, bind a bunch together to form a tight bundle. Working from the bottom, separate your branches as previously described in the steel control wire method, but twist all the strands together to form a tightly twisted stem, leaving the twiggy bits (that familiar arboreal term) sticking out as you go. Each branch can now be touched with a 12% flux and a 145 degree solder floated on. You will find that the solder will flow

very quickly and bond the wires together, so just a little touch with the hot iron will be all that is required. The same applies for the trunk of the tree; but a word of warning - make sure you have the right shape before binding up the trunk. Again, bark and the final finish is dealt with further on in the section.

Multi Gauge Wires

Why multi gauge? I find that by using various gauges of wire a more mature tree can be built quite quickly. This method is also governed by what is available in the scrap cable box, though a word with an electrician or a visit to an Electrical Wholesaler or larger DIY stores will be fruitful.

Starting with the main shape of the tree being modelled I find that for the best result, a skeleton or 'armature' - that is, the trunk - is made using the heaviest gauge of copper wire that can comfortably be worked. This 'armature' is very basic, and held together by a few twists of the wire, which is then either soldered or bonded by a few dabs of the hot glue gun, at strategic points. At the bottom of the armature I like to leave approximately 50-60mm of wire with some sheathing on, which is in turn stripped off and made into a root system on completion of the main tree. The species of tree and to an extent the season of the model, determine the number and density of branches. It seems to me to be a waste of time modelling a heavily foliated tree in high summer with all its minor branches and 'twiggery' if they are to be completely covered in leaves, so as I have mentioned before, I note the amount and density of leaves, and decide upon the time of year to be modelled, before proceeding with the next step.

Forming the Armature

Assuming it is autumn or early spring, and the tree will be unclothed, I proceed with a smaller gauge of wire, stripped of its outer sheathing, cut to a suitable length and twisted up to form the minor branches. These are then twisted onto the armature, and either soldered to the main

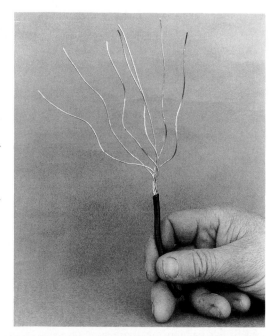

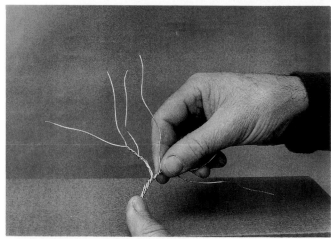

Top to bottom: progression of the basic copper wire canopy.

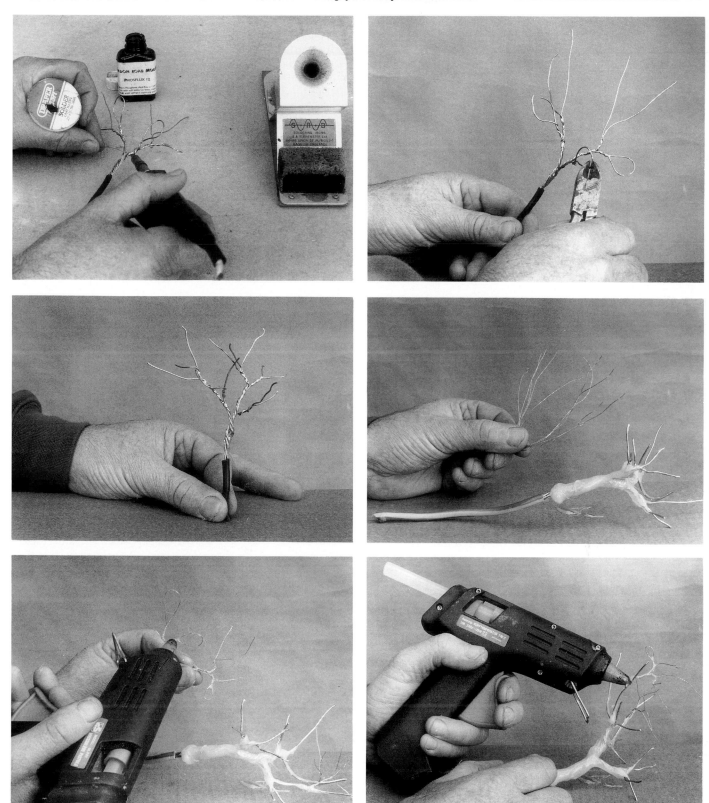

This page : stages in wire tree making, soldering on 'twists' and coating the wire with hot glue, to give thickening to the trunk and boughs.

stem or tacked with the hot glue gun. Each main branch is treated to several minor branches, until the required density is attained. I find it best to work from the bottom of the tree in an upward direction. These small twists of wire are themselves covered with further twists of finer wire, such as lighting flex worked up in a similar manner and then just touched with solder to bind the strands together. These are twisted onto the branch in turn and fixed.

If there are long forks left on the minor branches, I can put these to good use to form even more of the same, by turning the end back on itself and forming a loop, soldering up the joint and snipping the top of the loop, giving two branches for the price of one.

These smaller twists of wire are in themselves not unlike small trees or shrubs, and can be used as such if you find yourself with a few left over. I find it beneficial to leave approximately 30-

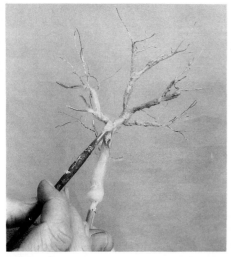

Painting on the plastermix to form bark.

Left: bare boughs, and bare plastermix, right: painted plastermix.

40mm of spare wire with its sheathing at the end of each twist, so the whole thing can be held whilst working with the soldering iron - copper wire becomes extremely hot, very quickly. Once the tree/shrub has been completed this sheathing can be stripped off and as mentioned previously, the wires spread to form a root system, which will aid the 'planting' of the tree on the 'ground'. It is also a good idea I find, to check on the shape of the tree by holding it up above the head, and looking up to the branches; if I have achieved a natural shape for the species, then I am happy. Bark? - coming soon.

Wire and Sisal Method

This method is a very old way of making trees and is especially useful when

length. Lay this flat and run some quick drying glue, such as UHU, down one limb. Cut some straight sisal strands to a length of approximately 50-60mm, and lay them onto the glued wire, making sure you have a fairly regular spread. Fold the other leg onto the 'branches' and set aside to dry - it is advisable to leave a small gap at the bend, to form a loop. This 'loop' is slid over a nail (driven into the workbench) with its head cut off to allow for the removal of the tree later. Insert the two ends of wire into a wheel brace/hand drill (not electric) and proceed to turn the drill for some eighteen revolutions. Remove the wire from the drill and slip the loop off the nail. Now you have something akin to a bottle brush, which can then be transformed into a tree by first of all snipping off the 'loop' close to the top of the tree, and with a pair of scissors cutting the branches to shape. Spray the whole thing afterwards with

be added. To my mind there are two ways of approaching this - one is to thicken up the trunk using an Artex or Rocks Galore (the last a modelling plaster from Set Scenes) pre-coloured mix, applied with a brush, and the other involves the use of a hot glue gun, applying the Artex/Rocks Galore mix on top. To take the first: start by washing the tree in very hot water and cheap (that is, without lanolin, which is worse than grease) washing up liquid, to degrease the copper wire, and paint the whole tree with neat PVA glue after reshaping the branches and twigs. As this is drying I mix up a slurry of either Artex or Rocks Galore, precoloured; add to this slurry a small amount of PVA glue, which aids the bonding of the plaster mix to the pre-coated copper wire. The slurry is of the consistency of thick cream and is applied using a No.7 or thereabouts paintbrush. Work all the branches first, then the main trunk of the tree, making sure that all twists of wire are covered. It is then set aside to dry. Once dry I proceed to add as many coats as is needed to get the required thickness of trunk and boughs. I've found that the more plaster mix is applied, the quicker it dries - a

Wire tree kit from Set Scenes.

representing conifers and similar types. It works well for 4mm and smaller, but is less effective in the 7mm and larger scales. Set Scenes do produce a pack for making them, the design of which goes back to the days of that great exponent of the art Jack Kine, and the following is really a description of his methods.

Assuming the scale is 4mm, cut a length of wire 16 inches long, bending it to an L shape, with the limbs of the L equal in

black spray paint. For bark - see next.

'Forming the Bark' and 'Hot Glue'

After the wire frame armature and all relevant branches and twigs have been assembled, the body/skin alias bark, can

Jack Kine development of a 'quick tree kit' from Set Scenes.

Old oak. Note undergrowth and bark texture. Openess of foliage with various shades of green.

Phew! Now make a model of this.

Weeping Willow.

phenomenon known as 'flash setting'. The final coats are the most important, for it is then that I give the tree its bark - having previously determined which type is involved. A plane for instance has a smooth, skin-like covering, whilst an oak, say, possesses a different order of roughness entirely. This latter appearance is achieved by stroking gently down the length of the trunk with a fairly coarse haired paintbrush, giving the effect of fissures. When painted with water colours they show to great effect.

The 'Hot Glue' method is a lot quicker and more robust. Begin by coating the tree using a hot glue gun; I like to use the multi-purpose glue sticks, working from the top of the trunk down all the main branches, leaving the smaller ones alone, building up a thicker trunk as I go by turning the tree around as the hot glue is applied. Remove the glue gun when the foot of the tree is reached, and continue to revolve it until the glue has cooled and set. If the tree is not quite the right shape then it can be twisted and bent without any damage being caused, allowing a truly realistic shape to be achieved. Once this happy stage has been reached then a coat or two of plaster mix, as previously described, will give the finishing touch. A word of warning here: do not try and bend the tree after the plaster mix has been applied...

Colouring - seeing the wood for the trees

The plaster mix when dry will readily take water colours or acrylics - consider the choice of colour well, for one wrongly coloured tree can stand out like a sore thumb, instead of blending in with its fellows. Water colours are my personal choice, I feel comfortable with them, and find the blending of colours a lot easier than acrylics. It is easier to start with a lighter colour and darken this as required, deciding first of all which side of the tree is likely to be north facing - add a hint of green to imitate moss and lichen. Brush up the darker water colours, using a No.7 brush, say; add lots of water - the paint will flow into the 'bark' fissures, highlighting them. When dry, add more. Once the overall finish is complete, add details such as ivy, squirrels, birds, snipers, giant gorillas or whatever. Dart Castings have a good range of such 'extras', to be found in good model shops. A convincing ivy can be added using a postiche carrier treated in the manner described soon after this section - Carriers 1, 2, etc.

Tree and Leaf

There is an endless variety to trees, and their foliage; almost any variety of technique could find a place somewhere so I will expand only on the materials that I think are the most likely to produce life-like foliage. We need to intercede on behalf of Nature here and invent something not yet evolved in the arboreal world. Between branch and leaf we need an intermediate stage - it is necessary, in most cases, to form a carrier, on which the foliage can be fixed. This foliage carrier in turn, with leaves affixed, is glued to the branches of the tree.

Foliage Carriers 1: Postiche

This is an artificial hair produced

This bark has been built up using layers of precoloured Rocks Galore from Set Scenes as described.

primarily for the theatre and film industry, brought to the modelling world by Jack Kine, and now supplied by Set Scenes. As a reminder, the stuff is also known as dolls' hair, or crepe hair, and comes in many 'hair colours' - red, blonde, black, brown, grey, ready packaged in useful plaited lengths. It produces a fine, almost invisible, backing for foliage when it is teased out. I have seen this material sold in Joke Shops, in straight lengths, and would advise you not to obtain it from such a source - the stuff seems permanently straightened and resists all attempts to impart a natural curve or curl.

Choose the right colour for your tree, a dark brown or black, pinch a piece off the end of the plait, an inch or so long, and proceed to tease this out into a light airy ball some two inches in diameter. Take a decent size of card as a backing or, say, the lid of a small box; pinch the ball into the corner of the box and spray with a 'firm hold' (it'll tell you on the can) unscented hairspray - the pump action type seems to be the most economical. The

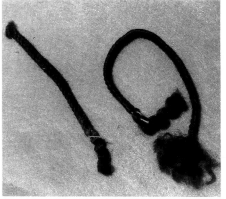

For the Luvvies - Postiche - a knot of 'theatrical hair'.

The nuts and bolts of foliage - scatter, postiche, hair spray.

Teasing out the postiche.

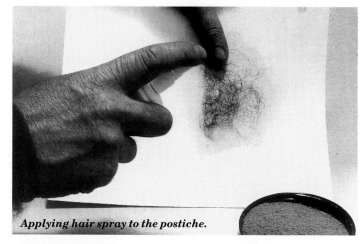

Applying hair spray to the postiche.

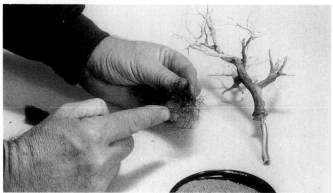

Postiche, saturated hair lacquer (you'll never view those British 1950s films the same way again).

Applying scatter material to the postiche by dipping in the pot.

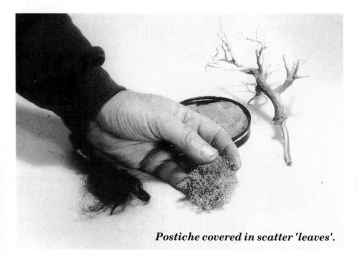

Postiche covered in scatter 'leaves'.

Summer comes at last. Applying the postiche and scatter to the tree.

Silver Birch 7mm scale.

card backing is to stop the hairspray from going all over the workshop, and will in some instances aid 'bounce back' onto the postiche. The fibres need to be thoroughly coated; when there are large globules of hairspray on the fibres, drop the sprayed postiche into a pot containing your chosen leaf material, turning it over gently and making sure that all the hair is covered by the scatter particles. Pick it out, shake off any loose particles, and set aside to dry naturally, or take a hairdryer and carefully blow dry the 'ball'. This is then laid to the branches of your tree. Now this 'ball' is quite fine, and heavy glue will spoil the finish, so, once the 'ball' is in place, and you are happy with the shape, spray the branch with hairspray or dilute PVA glue. The PVA glue must be well thinned, approximately 75% water and with the smallest drop of washing up liquid added - to break the surface tension of the water. I use an empty pump action hairspray container for this, and by working up and round the tree in this manner, you can produce a lightly foliated tree, with a realistically open canopy.

Foliage Carriers 2: Industrial Floor Cleaners and Scrubbers
I find that these materials can make for a 'heavier' tree. Begin by pulling or cutting small pieces of fibre from the discs - teased out and thinned in the process.

When happy with the shape, I spray with hairspray, following with a generous helping of scatter material, as already described in Foliage Carriers 1. By making several pieces at once, there is no waiting time involved when it comes to adding them to one's tree. As this material is denser than postiche, I find hot glue more appropriate for fixing the foliage to the branches, and working my way from the bottom branch of the tree, gluing on each piece carefully, can be a very rewarding process, as the shape of the tree becomes apparent. Look down on to the top of the tree and from underneath to check the shape is correct.

Foliage Carriers 3: Rubberised Horsehair
This material has been around for a long while and was originally used for packaging and for the stuffing in armchairs; it is now less common, but is still widely used in the modelling world. The method for employing it is the same as mentioned in Foliage Carriers 2, but spraying first with a matt black gives a better finish to the tree in general.

Foliage Carriers 4: Polyester Sheets
This is a fine 'airy' material and is treated in the same way as postiche - it comes precoloured as supplied by Greenscenes or in white, as currently supplied by Set Scenes. Woodland Scenics also supply this material, usually in a box with their white metal tree kits.

Leaves
There are several ways I have found of creating leaves and the methods are as follows:

Various scatter products.

Scatter Material
Formed of a precoloured crushed latex material graded in coarse, medium and fine granules. At the time of writing Set Scenes, Carrs and Greenscenes are the only producers known to me that produce conveniently sized packets. Alongside these are the ready foliated mats of the Woodland Scenics and Heiki ranges. I have found various other types that look similar and are widely available but have been disappointed with the results because, in my experience at least, they do not seem to be colourfast, fading very quickly. The aforementioned products, from Set Scenes/Greenscenes and Woodland Scenics seem to be wholly compatible with each other, and can be fixed with hairspray ('firm hold'), or watered-down PVA glue.

A mix of similar shades and grades is used to create foliage for trees or shrubs. There seems to be an infinite range of shades produced by the manufacturers, so creating life-like models should not be a problem. By mixing small amounts for your chosen tree, a shade from each packet, in a container, and storing what is left in a glass jar with a screw lid, it is possible soon build up a good 'library' of foliage, which can serve as ground cover plants and grass as well as for trees.

Woodland Scenics are relatively limited in colour and texture, and although very good and used extensively throughout the hobby, the result can look like Woodland Scenics, rather than leaves on a tree. I think the reason is that modellers tend to be heavy handed with the material - laying the matting over the branches and the tree as a whole, rather than teasing the material out and breaking it up, then laying it onto the branches as described in the section dealing with postiche. Adding the various shades of scatter material, as stated previously, to the matting, after it has been applied to the tree, will help disguise this familiar product. I have covered the application of the scatter material in the section dealing with foliage carrier.

Sawdust Leaves
Sawdust is still used by some manufacturers, and is very popular, I think because of its price, but it will only yield relatively poor results - not only does it fade but it is not colourfast in the presence of some sprays and adhesives and is therefore best left alone.

If you are in any doubt about the type of material sold in Model/ Hobby shops ask your retailer if he knows

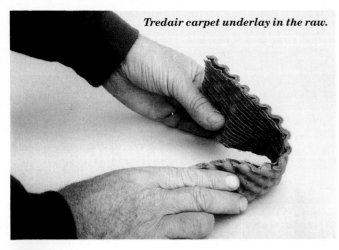

Tredair carpet underlay in the raw.

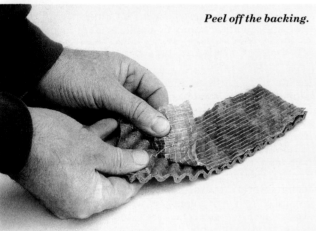

Peel off the backing.

Break into small pieces and put into coffee grinder.

A whizz with the grinder and Hey Presto, our own scatter material.

whether the material is colourfast, and if it is made of latex. If he has no idea then purchase a small packet, take it home, and spray it with hairspray or watered-down PVA glue; if the colour runs from the material then I suggest you give up on it.

Home-made Leaves - Latex Carpet Underlay
If you want to experiment with this

Alternative scatter from pot scourer - the process involves freezing - see text.

material, first of all may I suggest that you have a word with the domestic management and borrow a small coffee grinder and/or liquidiser - this will be essential equipment if you are to produce home-made leaves from carpet underlay.

I have recently found 'Tredaire' green underlay to be eminently suitable. Cut it into small pieces, say 12 inches square and peel off the hessian backing, then break up the green latex into small pieces approximately an inch square. Drop several into a small electric coffee grinder

and switch on for a few seconds, switch it off and let the particles settle, shake the grinder gently, switch on for a few more seconds, and then tip the fine particles out. I won't say Hey Presto, but there should be a nice pile of foliage ready for use. Although not as fine and refined as the products mentioned earlier, it is a very useful medium.

Home-made Leaves - Foam Backed Pot Scourer
Everyone has an ancient pot scourer, the type that is squarish with a coarse scouring face to it, sold in pairs in your local shop or supermarket. Peel off the scouring face, soak the foam in an emulsion paint (slightly thinned) of your chosen colour, squeeze out most of the

paint, allow it to dry and then freeze it. Once frozen pop this into a liquidiser and chop it up, and for a final chop pop it into the coffee grinder. I take no responsibility for the domestic consequences of this process - it might well be better carried out clandestinely...

And even - Real 'Leaves'
Used teabags, once dried, have proved very useful for portraying dead leaves and can be fixed with neat PVA glue directly to the twigs of trees, or scattered around the base of trees, hedgerows and shrubs. The loose leaf teas have a larger section and can be coloured using watered down emulsion paints, achieved by mixing the emulsion in a suitable receptacle and soaking the leaves in it overnight. Tip out the remaining paint through a strainer and dry the leaves, making sure that none stick together. It may well be a useful tip to try soaking some leaves in an Indian ink of a suitable colour and leaving to dry. The application of the leaves is described in the section dealing with postiche and the various carriers.

Chapter Six
WATER, WATER, EVERYWHERE

There is no gentle way of putting it, but the truth is, the successful and convincing modelling of water probably demands more time and patience than any of the techniques previously discussed. I have attempted different ways of representing water, over many years, but have found really only two approaches to be effective, and I will concentrate on these. Water has played a large part in the formation of any scenery, so I believe it should be portrayed somewhere on our model, in the form of either a drainage ditch, puddle, stream, small pond, river, estuary, seaside or whatever. Running water has always been difficult but a good representation can be achieved with practice. A small stream running over rocks is a very attractive feature, whilst a calm pond reflecting its surroundings adds an incalculable dimension for the viewer. If the water is clear, added details underwater really bring things to life. My two approaches are: straight

layer upon layer of varnish with detail painted on every coat or, if deep water is to be represented, a layer of clear acrylic sheet with details beneath, coated with varnish on the top surface along with extra details added, such as lily pads.

The odd island adds to general milieux.

A Good Bed

Having decided where the water body is to be on my landscape, I like to start with a good solid foundation, made of something like plywood, a stable material which can be fixed level relatively easily using PVA glue and screws. This is very important, for if there are lows (and corresponding highs) they will always show in the finish, unless you do a good filling job to bring up the levels. If the thing is out of level, of course, the finishing coats will always run to the lowest point, just like the real H2O.

I cut plywood some 60-70mm wider than the river or pond bed, allowing an overhang for fixing. I use a power jig-saw, or a padsaw, two tools which make it easy to cut out almost any shape that is needed. If for any reason the baseboard is uneven, I find it easier at this point to level up the bed with packing, such as pieces of cardboard or slithers of wood, wedged and trapped in the

Don't forget the everyday item on your model - the rope and tyre kids swing from would be another...

Small ripples and reflections will create a stunning effect.

Fast moving water forced between 'brick banks' a common feature and very satisfying to model.

Water meadows afford excellent opportunity for randomly putting features onto your surface.

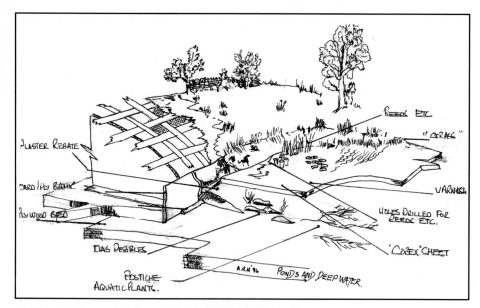

relevant places. I then glue and screw the bed into place using good one inch No.8 countersunk screws.

Once the bed is laid, I start to form the banks, either from thick, good quality cardboard, or a thin 3mm plywood. These are then bedded in with a suitable adhesive - applying beads of hot glue with the gun, to seal the joint almost instantly. If a bead is left on the water side of the bank it can be disguised with 'mud', made from a precoloured plastermix.

The 'foundations' then, consist of a plywood bed, securely fixed and level, with the banks made of a thin ply or a good quality thickish cardboard, sealed now with a coat of PVA glue. I then mix Artex with powder paint to the required shade, mixed in turn with PVA glue and water, painted on and worked into every corner and crevice of the banks and beds, lightly brushing out any deep brush strokes on the bed. When I am working on the bed I stipple

polyurethane varnish into the wet plastermix - water and varnish will react against each other and when dry will give a realistic 'crazing', adding to the overall effect.

Having made the bed, I then proceed with either of the following methods, depending on the water feature I require.

Deep Water

To achieve the desired effect, the deepest point of a pond or lake is coloured with darker shades - start with under water detail at a suitable distance from the bank. Detail around the edges such as reeds and bullrushes are added later.

Rocks can be made from small pieces of DAS - I flatten them before sticking them down, usually in clusters on the bed. On the surface they are more rounded and are added after all other work has finished. Any undulations in the bed are formed with Artex, suitably coloured as described earlier in this chapter. Whilst the plaster is still wet I like to add various pieces of foliage, from various materials such as sisal string coloured with Indian inks, or postiche treated with hairspray and scatter material, as described in the chapter on trees. All these items are pressed (planted) into the wet plastermix and sprayed with hairspray. Working fairly swiftly, I cut a piece of acrylic sheet, such as Cobex, to the required size and shape. The sketches will show how I bed this in, but I will endeavour to set the scene with words. Allowing a gap of about 10 or 20mm between the underside of the sheet and the bed, I form a rebate in the bank to sit the sheet on, by coating the Cobex on the underside with Vaseline (to act as a releasing agent) where it comes in contact with the Artex. The plastermix is spread around the perimeter and while still fairly thick, work the banks to form the correct contours. The 'sheet water' is pressed into the banks until it is level and flat - clean off any plaster that has spread onto the top of the surface, then leave to dry in a warm room.

After all is dry, I carefully cut around the edge and release the sheet with a scalpel or craft knife. The dried plaster mix will have a rebated edge which is then painted with the required colours. Some attention to the underside of the sheet water is now required, and with a tissue I wipe away any traces of the Vaseline, then lay this back on the rebate and mark with a felt tip pen where I think rushes and marginal plants might be, and any underwater plants that may be close to the surface. These are painted onto the underside of the Cobex sheet, using various shades of water colours - greens, blues, yellows, browns- carefully dabbing the nearly dry brush onto the surface. When all the painting is finished and dry, a coat of varnish is applied to serve as a seal. Now for the marginals - these are planted into the 'sheet' water by drilling

Bed with rebate formed.

Working up the bank detail.

Aquatic plants 'bedded down'.

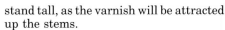

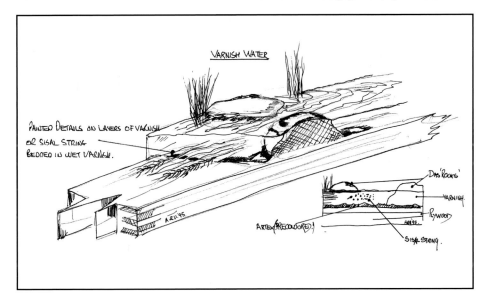

SMALL BRICK CULVERT.

stand tall, as the varnish will be attracted up the stems.

Represent such surface plants as lilies by either a dab of thick matt enamel or acrylic paints. I have even used tissue paper cut into the right shape and stuck down.

Streams and Running Water

Forming A Good Bed as described earlier, I try to create the illusion of running water by painting on many coats of varnish, with each coat allowed to dry before adding the next. If any detail is required in the water I just add these between coats - long trailing water plants for instance are formed from precoloured strands of sisal string laid on the wet varnish and allowed dry with it. The

Note aquatic plants laying with the flow and dead plants on bank behind bridge.

several holes, as close to each other as my thick and fumbly carpenter's fingers will allow. The plants are then pushed through the holes and sealed with UHU glue, neat PVA or even varnish, whatever is handy at the time. The making of reeds follows after the next section. Once this Cobex sheet of water is detailed with reeds, aquatics and so on, I set the whole thing back in its position with PVA glue

and disguise the boundary between the banks and the water. Using one of the methods described earlier for grass, either carpet tufts, or hairy underlay, cut into small strips, I glue the 'grass' over the joins (see photos). Bringing the dry and coloured grass onto the edge of our sheet of water renders the boundary invisible. Varnish the whole area, being very careful around the edges of where the plants

dodge is repeated on the next coat, staggering the position of the string so as to give the illusion of depth to our stream course. The same principle is employed if painting on the aquatic plants. Using water colours on a nearly dry brush, and starting with a darker shade, work toward the top coat using progressively lighter shades, staggering each layer as you go. Rocks, if they are to project above

Running water always looks interesting.

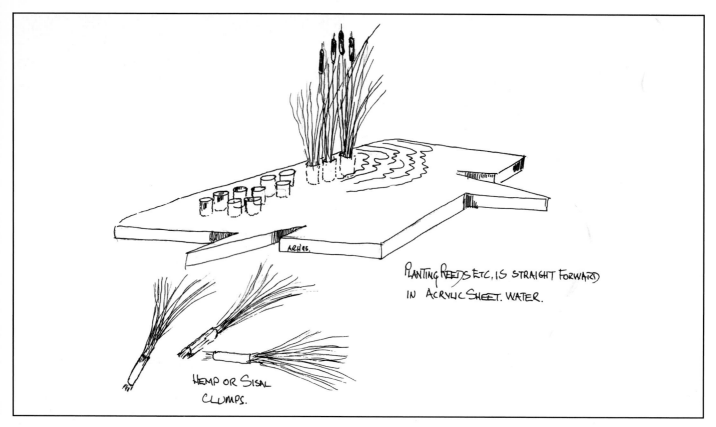

PLANTING REEDS ETC, IS STRAIGHT FORWARD IN ACRYLIC SHEET. WATER.

HEMP OR SISAL CLUMPS.

the water surface, can be planted after the varnishing has been finished - again these are fashioned from DAS rolled and sculpted into shape, painted and stuck down with either a dab of hot glue or UHU. If the pebbles, cobbles and boulders (let's use a bit of proper scientific description) are to remain below the water surface, they can be formed in the river/stream bed before the varnish is applied.

Where water is forced through a narrow gap or in a thin layer, over a stony bed for instance, the rushing water can become white to the eye as bubbles form and the water 'foams'. To achieve this 'white

water' effect in model form I dab water colour (white!) into the wet varnish, moving it around in the oily surface, letting it dry. I find several coats of this treatment works well, and to add even more detail between each coat of oil varnish, I add a coat of acrylic varnish (satin finish or eggshell) and when this is nearly dry I drag a fairly coarse bristled paintbrush through, to give the illusion of rushing water. This dries very quickly in a warm room and therefore takes up little time. There is, incidentally, an acrylic gel available from Set Scenes - when applied in a similar manner it convincingly replicates ripples and waves

and will dry where it is placed without any subsequent spreading.

Reeds/Bullrushes

At the water's edge where it is shallow and still, there will (generally) be reeds, bullrushes and similar plants. To simulate these in model form is a relatively simple process, which involves a witches' brew of plumbers' hemp, sisal string strands or bristles of a discarded dust brush, PVA glue, and water or enamel paint. Methodology is as follows - cut off a suitable length of a few strands of sisal string or plumbers hemp, take half a dozen of these strands and dip one end

Marginals - Iris, Marsh Mayold etc. - note deepening effect of light.

Lock of sisal, unprototypically placed in our landscape.

Glueing the base of our sisal marginals. Note - we have two 'plants' - glued in the middle.

Rolling ends between thumb and forefinger.

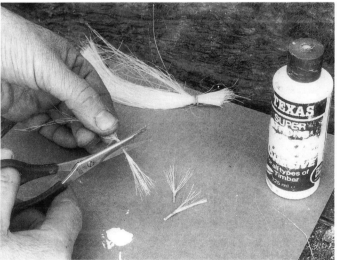

Cutting the 'tap root', to give two plants.

into neat PVA glue. Roll this between thumb and forefinger until all the strands have been coated, roll it further and then lay it on a piece of newspaper to dry, repeating the process until there are enough clumps. Apply water colour and leave to dry; they're then 'planted', either in the soft plastermix of the 'water margin', or in pre-drilled holes in the acrylic sheet of the 'water body' - in the latter case sealing the hole with a dab of PVA glue or varnish. Once all the holes are filled, I tease up some of the strands; others I curl down, for that little extra 'true to life' detail.

Larger plants such as bullrushes are formed from bristles cut from a brush, and inserted into the holes along the side of the sisal/hemp strands. I dab the top end of the bristle with neat PVA glue to simulate the bullrush seed head, then paint this a dark brown.

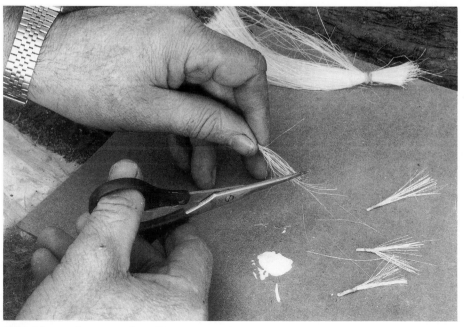

Trimming to the correct length.

Left:- Retaining walls etc. Note the dressed edges and corners and the overhanging vegetation - a good and interesting feature for modelling.

Right:- Vertically laid stones to form 'cockup' or copings. Photo Peter Barnfield.

Left:- Dartmoor drystone wall in advanced state of senescence. Note the horizontal courses and infills, long- dead bracken and green shoots breaking through.

The odd brick wall, covered in ivy and vegetation, lends a touch of realism to your model.

Chapter Seven
WALLS AND HEDGES

(There are very many good 'ready to run' fencings and brick wallings on the market, in almost bewildering variety - in many cases even individual pre-Grouping companies are separately represented. These I've not included, this being a 'how to' book.)

Dry Stone Walls

Where I live, in the south east corner of Kent, there are very few dry stone walls, so when in parts of the country where they proliferate, I find myself constantly marvelling at the skills of the waller, working his way up and over hills and mountains. In Scotland the walls are known as 'dikes' and there, as in most upland areas, I have noticed that even quite severe slopes do not seem to have inhibited the wallers, though in this sort of situation they are far less likely, now, to be strictly maintained.

The skill to build them has long been in decline but I will describe something of how they are put up. The wall is usually wider at the base than the top, and is laid without the aid of any mortar; the stones are usually collected from the immediate area round about, and left in piles at intervals determined by eye, for the waller will know how many stones he will need for a given distance. Foundation stones are laid in a shallow trench, having their most even edges facing outwards. Stones slope slightly downward to the centre of the wall, and gaps in the outer 'skins' are filled with small pieces - known as 'hearting'. At regular intervals a 'through stone' or 'throughs' are laid across the full width of the wall to form a tie between the two outer skins. Once the required height is reached the wall is 'coped' or 'topped off' with vertically placed slate-like stones. These are carefully chosen for their shape and regular size. These are commonly known (and I've checked again, at the publisher's instigation) as er, 'cockups'. It is usual in some areas to leave the ragged size of the copings protruding towards a neighbour's land.

Interesting features often found in these walls are the crossing points; known as 'hog holes' or just 'holes', they allow sheep and other grazing animals to pass from field to field. Stiles are also formed for us human beings, large horizontal slabs which wear concave with generations of feet. These little details will make interesting cameos...

Dry stone walls from faced-off card

This method requires a hot glue gun, fairly stout quality cardboard of good quality, about eighth of an inch in thickness and DAS or artex/ Rocks Galore plastermix (precoloured of course) as well as PVA glue, palette knife, a sharp scribing tool, a pair of compasses which will hold a pencil or lead, scalpel or craftknife, and watercolour paints.

I usually cut a strip of card which will represent the heart of the wall, the height of which is determined after I have scribed the bottom edge to fit the contours of the landscape. This is done by holding the card on the highest point of the landscape on the line of the wall and, setting a pair of compasses to the gap between the bottom of the card and the lowest point of the landscape. I then draw the compasses up and along the landscape until I have a line which follows the contours. I remove the card from the landscape and lay it flat, and cut along the line I have drawn with the compasses. I then mark the required height of wall - by setting the compasses to the correct distance, putting the point on the cut edge of the card and drawing it along, following the contours. Cut along this line.

When all is ready, I bed the card into a bead of hot glue, careful to keep fingers away. When the glue has set and the card is upright I then paint the entire length with PVA glue and coat the card with either a

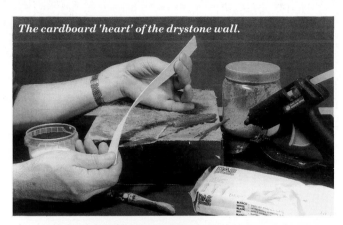
The cardboard 'heart' of the drystone wall.

Tacking down the pre-cut, scribed 'heart'.

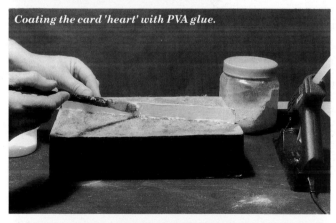
Coating the card 'heart' with PVA glue.

Pressing small pieces of DAS into the wet PVC.

Buttering the card heart with a precoloured plastermix.

Second step - 'scribing' the stone 'courses'.

The result.

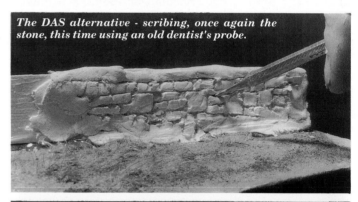

Fourthly - brush carefully for weathering. Don't put the brush back in the bathroom.

Coming along nicely.

The DAS alternative - scribing, once again the stone, this time using an old dentist's probe.

Toothbrush to the fore again, as with the plastermix approach.

The end result. There seems to be no great advantage, between plastermix and DAS, except maybe time - DAS is quicker. Both look subtlely different, so maybe it's a question of personel aesthetics.

precoloured plastermix or small pieces of DAS pressed into the glue and smoothed out to a thinnish regular surface. Whichever method is used I make sure that the top edge of the wall and both sides are well covered and sound, leaving all to dry before proceeding to the next stage.

I now draw with a pencil the position of the stones, using photographs as a guide,

doing a small area at a time, but making sure there are no vertical straight joints in the stonework, and the courses or horizontal joints run fairly consistently along the wall, in a similar way to brickwork, something known as bonding. A sharp pointed tool (the one I favour is an old dentist's probe filed to a bevelled point - see sketch) gives a roughish score

mark, which if pressed hard enough will break the edges and the corners of the 'stone', and when painted shows up rather well as weathered, individual stones.

When all the scribing is complete, I take my old toothbrush and scrub gently over the whole area, which serves two purposes - the first is to remove all

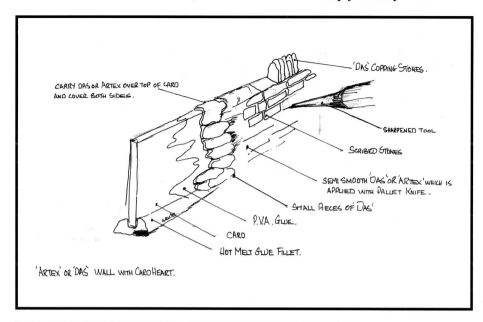

'Artex' or 'Das' Wall with Card Heart.

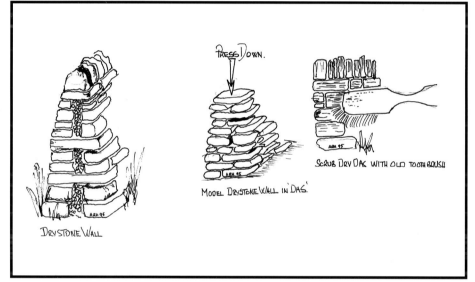

Drystone Wall

Model Drystone Wall in 'Das'.

Scrub Dry Das with Old Toothbrush!!

pressing them gently into the glue before they dry. For 7mm scale, I build two 'skins' of the wall as it were, with a bond and through stones placed at regular intervals, but in 4mm scale I use just one skin and carefully build up the wall until I reach the desired height (see sketches and photos). Once the height has been attained, I take a palette knife and pat the face sides, pushing down from the top to compress the 'stones' into a flatter configuration. Dab a little water on the wall with a paintbrush, just to dampen the DAS, as it does tend to dry fairly quickly when being handled by warm fingers. I always try and portray the 'rake' of the wall if at all possible, letting it lean 'into the contour', and to look a little tipsy here and there - an aspect which certainly comes about over time in the case of the real world. A dead straight, vertical dry stone wall doesn't look right, and remember that collapsing, neglected, abandoned and degraded ('unadopted' if you like) walls have long been common, in some areas they are more in evidence than properly maintained walls - and this has been the case for years.

Drying time of DAS in this situation is quite quick, but I find it can be aided by leaving it in a warm room overnight. When it is dry I proceed to brush over the whole surface with a toothbrush as mentioned previously - as DAS is a relatively soft clay it will give a real weathered appearance. Again the 'copings' or 'cockups' can be added as described previously, but for a little more realism in 7mm scale, a light brushing with a toothbrush in an up and down motion really enhances the grained effect of stone - and when painted it certainly comes to life.

Retaining Walls

These very common features have recently come to my notice on disused railways, where there are over-bridges and occupational crossings for farmers. These are invariably constructed in brick or stone - as the latter material is the one under consideration here, I will leave brick alone. (There are many good

unwanted bits left behind during the scribing and the second to give a convincing texture or 'grain' to the face of the stonework. Be very careful here as I have found on several occasions that the face will sometimes break away if brushed too hard. When this stage is complete and I am generally happy with the overall effect, I start to add the 'cockups' or 'copings'. These I make from small pieces of DAS rolled into a small ball then pressed flat and, depending on size, cut in half. I lightly coat the top edge of the wall with PVA glue, then with a pair of tweezers and the old dentist's probe, lay the stones vertically along the top of the wall. Once the stones are in position, I gently press the bottom edge into the glue so a bond is formed. If I have used DAS for the whole wall rather than plaster, then by damping the DAS copings and the top edge of the wall a bond will be achieved without PVA glue. The aforementioned operations, I have to say, are very tricky and patience-sapping, but

the end results are well worth the effort. I will deal with painting later on in this chapter.

Dry stone walls using DAS

DAS, being an air drying modelling clay, is very easy to use, and by pinching off a smallish piece from the main block (remembering to reseal the packet after opening each time) it is easy to form balls, about the size of a small pea, by rolling between the thumb and forefinger. As this dries fairly quickly I only make a small number at a time, laying these rough spheres in a bed of PVA glue to form the foundation, or footings and

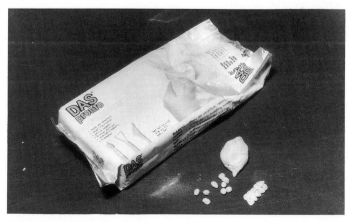

DAS and the rolled pellets - see over.

The 'drystone' wall begins.

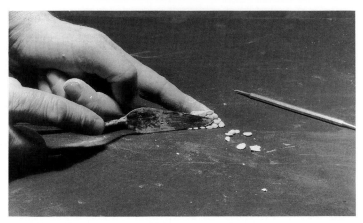

Small and fiddly, but worth the effort.

Finally, the er, cockups.

a colour such as black, and let the water take the pigments into the joints and fissures in the stonework. Once all this has dried I can see the detail and begin to pick out, with various shades of colour, the individual stones. Starting at the bottom of the wall, I use greens and browns, working up using lighter shades as I go. The reason for starting with darker shades at the bottom of the wall is to portray a damp, lichen covered stonework. Along the top edges, where the coping stones stand and intersect with the main wall, small traces of green paint are added at various intervals, to highlight the weathering effect where water has run off the top and down the outside. If I want to continue working on the wall I use a hairdryer to dry the face as quickly as I can, by playing a gentle heat across the surface, and then continue to add more colours in quick succession, blending them as I go with a drier brush. Once I have completed painting the wall, and I am happy with the general appearance, I fix the colours by an application of hairspray - not too much mind, just a light coating.

embossed card and plastic card versions of brick, and even books which describe their use - a visit to any medium sized exhibition will begin to reveal the enormous range and variety.) The stonework is cut and dressed in regular shapes, then laid in a formal pattern which is a challenge to model, to obtain those clean cut lines, but I find that by following my previously described procedures for the cardboard heart walls with DAS or plastermix coatings, a pleasing finish is achieved, with one extra element to add - the sharp-dressed vertical corners. These are created by using a straight edge and scalpel, the straight edge laid against the external corner and the scalpel or craftknife drawn carefully down the straight edge. A light brushing with the old toothbrush completes the task. Where arches are formed then a card template is laid in the arch, and a pair of dividers are used to scribe a sharp edge to the dressed stone, by opening out the dividers to the correct radius and striking an arc around the edge of the stone.

Painting

Plastermix is best used precoloured, for it gives a basecoat from which to work. It is from this base colour that I add the darker colours to give contrast and depth. Where I have used DAS to build my wall, I will start by flooding the whole wall with

Neatly trimmed hedge with trees. Sycemore and Oak further down the lane.

The old layered hedge trimmed back many times - come the summer it will be bursting with leaves.

The minimal hedge.

Hedges

Hedgerows are more common where I live, and it has to be said I take them for granted, but looking more closely in recent years I have noticed their many varied forms. In open countryside owners

erosion and other deleterious effects are manifest - now, though the trend to eliminate hedges may at least be slowing (or even reversing in some instances) even in the stronghold of the English hedged field, Devon, some scarring continues, to

I set to by cutting out, with a strong pair of scissors, my chosen sub base. Favoured material is the disc type floor scrubber, as mentioned elsewhere in this book. I favour the black one, as it is coarser, and requires no colouring. It is

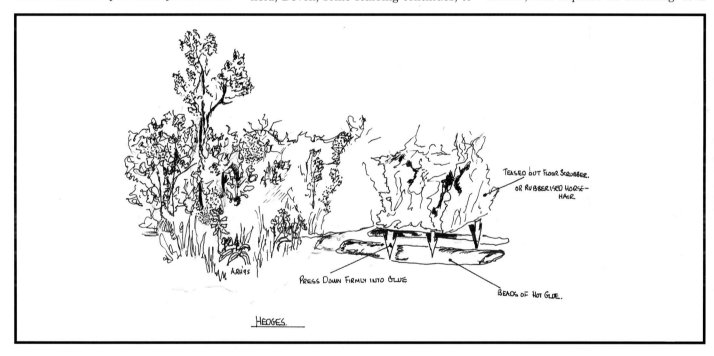

HEDGES.

seem more minded to 'let them go' and they form small trees rather than a close, tight hedgerow that has been clipped. Where the trees have grown, the farmer will string wire fencing between the trunks, adding to this open quality, but alongside roads and tracks, hedges tend to be closely cut and well maintained, forming a dense growth. Generally made up of hazel, hornbeam, willow, and hawthorn, bushes such as blackberry also grow amongst them. 'Prairiefication' proceeds (most notoriously in East Anglia, but in many other parts of the country) as hedgerows are grubbed out aided, absurdly, by taxpayers' money for many these past years. Yet as farmers have discovered in recent years, where 'prairie' farming has become more common, soil

this day. A concern for the hedge is growing, along with the planting of sapling trees to form copses in the corners of fields, and these, and their historical precedents, make for excellent cameos on our landscape models.

Hedges in summer

I have to admit to using hedges to cover all manner of half modelled details, an unfinished wall, for instance, converted into a hedge - not so unlike, after all, the real thing. Using rubberised horsehair, industrial floor scrubbers, postiche, scatter material and copper wire, and armed with the ubiquitous photos and sketches, along with the good old hot glue gun, I have great fun in forming 'summer' hedgerows.

teased out to the shape required, which though it need not be too neat, should be fairly flat along the bottom edge. If I am unable to obtain a black disc I will use rubberised horsehair, which needs to be coloured by spraying with a matt black paint. It can be one of the car paint products or I sometimes use my airbrush and spray it with enamels. I reckon to use a black paint as this becomes less obtrusive when the hedge is complete, but having said that, there are areas where a lighter sub-base would enhance the general appearance.

Once I have teased out and obtained my general shape, I glue this down with my hot glue gun, which is then treated with a liberal coat of either hairspray or watered down PVA glue, 25% PVA glue to

Rubberised horsehair and (left) floorscourer.

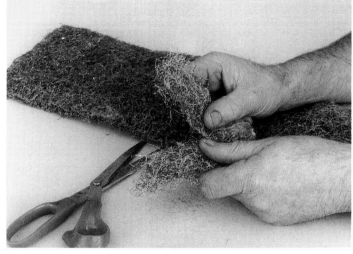

Tearing the rubberised horsehair into 'hedge size' pieces. I get the variation so characteristic of hedges by making them in bits, not the linear pieces you might expect - not that the latter doesn't work too...

Spraying rubberised horsehair/floorscourer hedge sub-base with hair spray...

... when saturated, sprinkle on scatter material.

Poised to glue down the hedge to the baseboard using hotglue gun or chosen adhesive.

Hedge, finally, in position.

75% water. I then sprinkle various shades of scatter materials, either leaving to dry naturally or hurried along with the hairdryer, set on a gentle heat. Where I need to portray various species of shrubs, then I will use postiche, teased out and treated in the manner described in the 'hug a tree' chapter. If I need to show a small tree growing out of the top of a hedge, this is then formed with copper wire, again as described under matters arboreal.

Hedges in winter

Follow the summer methods above, but don't add scatter material - I also tend to use teased out (actually extremely well thinned out) rubberised horsehair. This 'extra thinned' material is supported with twisted copper wire, treated in the same manner as described for making trees, and planted in the centre of the hedgerow. The odd evergreen shrub, such as holly, is added for 'depth'.

The Hedge Base

At the base of all hedges there is undergrowth - nettles, docks, thistles, long grass, ground elder, and so on. I portray these by using sisal string, jute and carpet underlay (hairy kind) and small tufts of green carpet. To form nettles and similar tall standing plants, I cut sisal string to the required length and dip these strands into PVA glue, flicking the string with a finger to knock off any excess of glue. These strands are then dipped into a fine scatter material of my chosen colour, and set aside to dry. If the hedge has been planted directly onto the hairy carpet underlay grass, then I will choose an area where the 'nettles' are to be planted, and close crop the grass. I proceed to push small holes with a screwdriver (or similar tool) into the sub base, then with a dab of glue and a pair of tweezers, plant the strands of sisal string. Working my way along the hedgerow, I will tease up some of the hairs from the carpet underlay and spray these with hairspray, and (sparingly) sprinkle fine scatter material over the top to simulate some of the wild flowers. The modeller as the bringer of plenty.

LAYED HEDGE (COPPER WIRE TWISTED TOGETHER AND PLANTED IN ROWS.)

Right:- The 'undergrowth' here is used with a micro-plastic strip fence to give depth to the scene.

Chapter Eight
CONCLUSION
A few scenes from my layout 'Wigleton' - photos Len Weal.

Having ploughed (good landscape modelling image, that) your way this far, I do hope you have found this little exposition both useful and maybe, even, inspirational. It has been quite an exercise for me, trying to remember all the little tricks and dodges that I have long taken for granted, and it is only now, compiling this book, that I realise just how many there are. I hope I have got enough of them across, and in a (more or less) comprehensible way. Landscape modelling has really come a long way in the last few years, and long may it continue. Good luck with your modelling and enjoy your creations.

Landscape and Scenic Aids Suppliers
Set Scenes PO Box 63 Crawley, West Sussex RH11 8YR
Greenscene 60 Hollymount, Worcester WR4 9SF
Carrs Modelling Products, 528 Kingston Road, Raynes Park, London SW20 8DT
Polystyrene Cutter Proops Educational Packages, Unit 24, Fiddlebridge Ind. Centre, Lemsford Road, Hatfield, Herts, AL10 DE

Useful Books
The Tree Book, by J Edward Milner ISBN 1-85585-132-6
The Ever-Changing Woodlands, Readers Digest, ISBN 0-276-37434-7
The Trees of Britain and Northern Europe, by Allan Mitchell & John Wilkinson ISBN 0-00-219857-6
The Photographic Guide to the Identification of Native & Common Trees, by Roger Phillips ISBN 0-241-11758-5
Woodland Trees and Shrubs, Readers Digest-National Trust ISBN 0-276-39291-4

Above:- Varnished 'water' in harmony with a 'scatter' moor.

Left:- A 'K' ro-rail bus trundles through the countryside - 'bliss absolute bliss'.

The branch line almost swamped by Mother Nature.

Scattercoat on lint has been used extensively here, with a tree foliage of Scattercoat on Woodlands Scenics, rubberised horse hair and copper wire tree trunks.

The tree behind the bridge is an old cedar, much abused. (Along with the pointing hitch-hiker).

A brave squirrel about to take on the might of the tank engine, sits on the ground frame box adjacent to the bridge parapet wall.